T0114255

SOUTH
to a
VERY OLD
PLACE

SOUTH

to a

VERY OLD
PLACE

by ALBERT MURRAY

Vintage Books
A Division of Random House, Inc.
New York

For my wife
MOZELLE
who, honeysuckle-fairytale downhome girl
that she is, was, as the old folks used to say,
born knowing

All rights reserved under International and Pan-American Copyright
Conventions. Published in the United States by Vintage Books, a division of
Random House, Inc., New York, and distributed in Canada by Random House
of Canada Limited, Toronto. Originally published in hardcover by
McGraw-Hill Book Company, New York, in 1971.

"Youth" by Langston Hughes. From *The Dream Keeper and Other Poems* by
Langston Hughes. Copyright © 1932 Alfred A. Knopf, Inc.; 1960 Langston
Hughes. Reprinted by permission of the publisher.

"Thrilled." Copyright © 1935 DeSylva, Brown and Henderson, Inc.;
1963 Chappell & Co., Inc.

"The Music Goes Round and Round" by Red Hodgson, Edward Farley and
Michael Riley. Copyright © 1935 Select Music Publications, Inc.;
1962 Anne-Rachel Music Corporation.

"The Little Things You Used to Do" (Warren Dubin). Copyright © 1935;
1963 M. Witmark & Sons. Used by permission of Warner Bros. Music.
All rights reserved.

Library of Congress Cataloging-in-Publication Data
Murray, Albert.
South to a very old place / by Albert Murray.—1st Vintage Books ed.
p.   cm.
Reprint. Originally published: New York : McGraw-Hill, 1971.
ISBN 978-0-679-73695-0
1. Afro-Americans—Alabama—Social life and customs.   2. Alabama—
Social life and customs.   3. Murray, Albert—Childhood and youth.
4. Afro-Americans—Alabama—Biography.   5. Alabama—Biography.
I. Title
[E185.93.A3M87   1991]
976.1'0049607302—dc20
[B]   91-50214
CIP

(Stoop) if you are abcedminded, to this claybook, what curios of signs (please stoop), in this allaphbed! Can you rede (since We and Thou had it out already) its world?It is the same told of all. Many. Miscegenations upon miscegenations.

JAMES JOYCE
Finnegans Wake

But lo, the world hath many centres, one for each created being, and about each one it lieth in its own circle. Thou standest but an ell from me, yet about thee lieth a universe whose centre I am not but thou art. . . . And I, on the other hand, stand in the centre of mine. For our universes are not far from each other so that they do not touch; rather hath God pushed them and interwoven them deep into each other, so that you . . . do indeed journey quite independently and according to your own ends, whither you will, but besides that you are the means and tool, in our interwovenness, that I arrive at my goal.

THOMAS MANN
Joseph in Egypt

The true ancestral line is not necessarily a straight or continous one.

W. H. AUDEN
Journal of an Airman

Not everything in this book is
meant to be taken literally. Some
names have been changed, some not.

CONTENTS

NEW YORK

Tall Tale Blue Over Mobile Bay in Harlem

You can take the "A" train uptown from Forty-second Street in midtown Manhattan and be there in less than ten minutes. There is a stop at Fifty-ninth Street beneath the traffic circle which commemorates Christopher Columbus who once set out for destinations east on compass bearings west. But after that as often as not there are only six more express minutes to go. Then you are pulling into the IND station at 125th Street and St. Nicholas Avenue, and you are that many more miles north from Mobile, Alabama, but you are also, for better or worse, back among homefolks no matter what part of the old country you come from.

But then, going back home has probably always had as much if not more to do with people as with landmarks and place names and locations on maps and mileage charts anyway. Not that home is not a place, for even in its most abstract implications it is precisely the very oldest place in the world. But even so, it is somewhere you are likely to find yourself remembering your way back to far more often than it is ever possible to go by conventional transportation. In any case, such is the fundamental interrelationship of recollection and make-believe with all journeys and locations that anywhere people do certain things in a certain way can be home. The way certain very special uptown Manhattan people talk and the way some of them walk, for instance, makes them homefolks. So whoever says you can't go home again, when you are for so many intents and purposes back whenever or wherever somebody or something makes you feel that way.

There is also the "D" train which you can take from Forty-second Street over on Sixth Avenue, because that way you still come into the "A" train route at Columbus Circle. Or you can take Number Two or Number Three on the IRT, and the uptown Avenue will be Lenox, and if you get off at 125th Street you walk west to the old Theresa Hotel corner at Seventh, the Apollo near Eighth, and Frank's Chophouse, on over toward St. Nicholas. At the 135th Street IRT stop you come out at the northwest corner of Lenox Terrace, and you are also at the new Harlem Hospital. From there, which is only a few steps from the AME Church that used to be the old Lincoln Theatre, you walk east to Riverton, Lincoln, and the water. But for the Schomberg Library, the YMCA poolroom, and Small's Paradise, you walk west toward the hill and CCNY.

Sometimes, of course, all you need to do is hear pianos and trumpets and trombones talking, in any part of town or anywhere else for that matter. Or sometimes it will be pianos and saxophones talking and bass fiddles walking; and you are all the way back even before you have time to realize how far away you are supposed to have gone, even before you become aware of even the slightest impulse to remember how much of it you thought perhaps you had long since forgotten.

Sometimes it can be downhome church organs secularized to Kansas City four-four in a neighborhood cocktail lounge. It can be a Count Basie sonata suggesting blue steel locomotives on northbound railroad tracks (as

4

"Dogging Around" did that summer after college). It can be any number of ensemble riffs and solo licks that also go with barbershops and shoeshine parlors; with cigar smoke and the smell and taste of seal-fresh whiskey; with baseball scores and barbecue pits and beer-seasoned chicken-shack tables; with skillets of sizzling mullets or bream or golden crisp oysters plus grits and butter; and with such white potato salads and such sweet potato pies as only downhome folks remember from picnics and association time camp meetings. Or it can even be a stage show at the Apollo Theatre which sometimes rocks like a church during revival time. It can be the jukebox evangelism of some third-rate but fad-successful soul singer (so-called) that carries you back not only to Alabama boyhood Sundays with sermons followed by dasher-turned ice cream, but also to off-campus hillside roadside beer joints and Alabama pine-needle breezes.

So naturally it can also be Lenox Avenue storefront churches, whether somewhat sedate or downright sanctified. Or it can be the big league uptown temples along and off Seventh Avenue: such as, say, Big Bethel, Mother Zion, Metropolitan, Abyssinian Baptist, where on the good days Adam Clayton Powell, for all his northern-boy upbringing, sounds like Buddy Bolden calling his flock.

None of which is to suggest—not even for one sentimental flicker of an instant—that being back is always the same as being where you wish to be. For such is the definitive nature of all homes, hometowns, and hometown people that even the most joyous of homecoming festivities are always interwoven with a return to that

5

very old sometimes almost forgotten but ever so easily alerted trouble spot deep inside your innermost being, whoever you are and wherever you are back from.

For where else if not the old home place, despite all its prototypical comforts, is the original of all haunted houses and abodes of the booger man? Indeed, was even the cradle only a goochie-goochie cove of good-fairy cobwebs entirely devoid of hobgoblin shadows; or was it not also the primordial place of boo-boo badness and doo-doo-in-diapers as well?

Once back you are among the very oldest of good old best of all good friends, to be sure, but are you not also just as likely to be once again back in the very midst of some snarled-up situation from which you have always wanted to be long gone forever?

And where else did you ever in all your born days encounter so much arrogant ignorance coupled with such derisive mockery and hey-you who-you crosstalk? Where else except in this or that Harlem are you almost always in danger of getting kicked out of a liquor store for instance for browsing too casually in the wine section. Where else except among homefolks is that sort of thing most likely to tab you not as an expense-account gourmet-come-lately but a degenerate wino? Or something worse.

But still and all and still in all and still withal if there are (as no doubt there have always been) some parts of Harlem where even such thugs and footpads as inhabited the London of Charles Dickens would probably find themselves more often mooched and mugged than mooching and mugging so are there at least one thousand plus one other parts and parcels also. Not to mention such browngirl eyes as somehow can always make even the smoggiest New York City skies seem tall tale blue over Mobile Bay.

Naturally there are those who not only allege but actually insist that there can only be ghetto skies and pathological eyes in Harlem and for whom blues tales are never tall but only lowdown dirty and shameful. But no better for them. They don't know what they're missing. Or don't they? For oh how their pale toes itch to twinkle as much to the steel blue percussion as to all the good-time moans and the finger-snapping grunts and groans in Billy Strayhorn's ellington-orchestrated nostalgia.

ONE

NEW HAVEN

Deposition for Two at Yale

You can also go south from midtown Manhattan by taking another northbound train from Forty-second Street: one going up beneath and then above Park Avenue. Take the Yankee Clipper, for instance, or the Merchants Limited, or the Bay State Special. But this time you keep on past 125th Street. This time you roll on across the Harlem River and continue on through the Bronx and that part of suburbia to Connecticut. Then one hour and maybe fifteen, maybe twenty, maybe thirty or thirty-five minutes later you are that many more statute miles further north from Mobile than Lenox Terrace, but you are also pulling into New Haven, where Yale has some very special downhome dimensions indeed these days. Nor are all of them derived from Yankee-shrewd concessions to militant civil rights rhetoric. There is Robert Penn Warren and there is C. Vann Woodward.

Because yes as seldom as such things are ever mentioned with longing, whing ding-doodle banjos and twang-nosed-talking–Jim-Crow-walking guitars and barnyard saw-fiddle music or any hints thereof even on a TV soundtrack can also take you back as rapidly as anything else. Even from Lenox Terrace. Because, after all, like it or not, or concede it or not, long before it became your boy-blue stamping ground the old country had already been old man whicker-bill's buckskin camping ground, back when it was still Indian territory.

So, what with somebody forever forgetting to turn the

radio off, you are carried back almost as often by such ragtime rooty-toot trumpets as used to talk confederate bugle talk above the two-beat razzmatazz of knock-down drag-out Saturday night roadhouses and moss-point casinos back when the best bootleg whiskey came from the sheriff's private stock. Yes there are also Harlem airshaft reverberations of all that too. So also such slow-dragging circus-tiger vibrato trombones as not only used to but still do tailgate such magnolia sundown sadness as is fit to test the patience of even the most gracious-seeming evil-tempered cooks and waiters and bellboys who ever shucked, stuffed, and took care of business on any steamboat or in any steamboat-gothic hotel—who could and still do endure it but not without badmouthing it to hell in the process: "Man ain't no goddam wonder so many of them people don't like nobody. Hump-the-goddam-hump dancing like that some of these sommiches bound to start whooping and hollering for somebody's blood and balls. Man, that music ain't getting nothing together."

Anyway all of that is also part and parcel of something else to which you are always returning without even going as far back south from Lenox Terrace as 110th Street: that interior benchmark site where things are still very much the same as they once were when you used to squint one of your whicker-bill–mocking eyes and stiffen the weather-beaten whicker-billness of your neck not only as if it were red-devil tootletoddle red but also as if it were wrinkled and stringy from too much tobacco chewing and so much white shirt-and-collar-and-tie wearing; standing with one foot forward and your whicker-bill elbows stuck out skinny, holding your back and shoulders as if you were just about to break into old man whicker-bill Charley Comesaw's bony butt, high instep strut as soon as the billygoat fiddles started sawing —that crackerjack gesture, however, being the whole joke, because as far as you were concerned just about the only white man who really knew how to strut his stuff walking back in those days was not anybody anywhere in and around or even near Mobile, Alabama. It was a western cowboy. It was the one and only Tom Mix walking neither pasty-faced nor red-necked but bowlegged; and then standing not like a flat-assed cracker deputy but hip-cocked and pointy-toed, with his thumbs hooked into his low-riding two-gun cartridge belt, his silk neckerchief knotted to one side, the angle of his ten-gallon western cowboy hat as sporty as a flashy-fingered piano player's gambling-hall fedora.

Nor did many things ever strike you as being more laughable than coming back down into the Saturday afternoon daylight of the Pritchard, Alabama, main street from the fabulous peanut-gallery darkness of King's Palace Theatre and seeing Pritchard, Alabama, white boys trying to act like Tom Mix (or Buck Jones or Fred Thompson or Ken Maynard)—and only looking more like whicker-bill peckerwoods than ever. How could Pritchard, Alabama, peckerwoods ever know what Tom Mix was all about?

All the same, all of them and all of that and more are no less warp and woof of what home on the outskirts of Mobile, Alabama, was also very much about. Which specifically includes all that which somebody who could

13

easily have been one of your up-north uncles or cousins Remus was talking about when he said to Quentin Compson: "You're right, they're fine folks. But you can't live with them"; which no doubt was the same situation on which some of the old heads by the fireside were musing when they used to come to the end of some story about somebody being in trouble, and mutter: "You got to know how to handle them; you got to outthink them, you got to stay one jump ahead of them"; but which so far as any number of others, old and young, yourself included, were concerned was a very good reason to un-ass the area. Not simply in flight, escape and hence abdication, however, but also in exploration, quest, and even conquest.

One snatch of either whingding or rooty-toot and even as you sit looking at the midtown Manhattan skyline from 132nd Street, looking south as you once did from the northward outskirts of Mobile, you are also back in the old spyglass place seeing all of them and that once more. But in better perspective, in proper complexity and with proper awareness of the ambiguity and ultimate obscurity of not just black and white motives down home but of all human motivation everywhere. Because after all that instantaneous, popeyed, no-matter-how-fleeting-expression of drawing-room outrage you register at the impropriety of all that old narrow-nosed, shaggyheaded blue-eyed talk when you hear it outside the South is perhaps as much an expression of kinship as of aginship whether you can admit it or not. Because if one part of your reaction is supercilious another is quite obviously interwoven with nothing so much as having to witness homefolks cutting a "country hog" in town, among strangers. Interwoven with something else also: a grudging admiration in spite of yourself because suddenly you also have to realize that if such talk did cut a hog, the scandal was either intentional or was likely to become defiantly so as soon as there was any hint that the hog cutting was being noted.

So, with however much ambivalence, yes them too: and besides sometimes what they represent as much as anything else is an old familiar difference and even a similar otherness, which is sometimes, especially in situations outside the South, even familiar when other: "Man goddamn where the hell these white folks come from? Man, these some of your goddamn white folks? Man, who the goddamn hell white folks these?"

And no less for all the trouble so many of them represent either. Because wherever and whenever downhome tales tall or otherwise are told, some of the very best are always about all of that too, and there is as much bragging about the extent and intensity of the obstacles, the conflicts, and the showdowns as about anything else, probably more (certainly more than either propriety or hipness will permit about any poon-tang conquest, for instance): "Man, you ain't seen no bad-assed crackers like them bad-assed crackers we had down my way. Man, I'm talking about some mean and gentlemen I mean some sure enough mean-ass peckerwoods. I'm talking about some hoojers so goddamn mean and evil they breathe like rattlesnakes. Man, hell, what you talking about is just some old pore-assed white-assed damn trash. I'm talking about some bad-assed peckerwoods,

15

and you better believe it. You ain't never in your born days seen no bad-assed crackers like them bad-assed crackers we had where I come from. You know them crackers around Bay Minette, Alabama, and on down toward Flomaton and into that old pineywoods country down in North Florida; you know how bad them dried-up-assed rosum-chewing squint-eyed crackers looking like they always sighting down a gun barrel at you, used to be out around Leaksville, Missippi, and all out through in there? Sheeeet, man, them old crackers ain't nothing to these old goddamn crackers I'm talking about!"

Yes alas and alas, the also and also of all them and that all of that, plus much more; and furthermore "what clashes here of wills gen wonts," which is to say shaggy-heads versus woollyheads much the same, alas, as if they were still "oystrygods gagging fishygods" has never been any less familiar than all the rest and best of it.

The one that Robert Penn Warren looks and walks and talks like is not old man Whicker-Bill Comesaw, but Red Scarborough in the old Texaco filling station out on old Telegraph Road. As for C. Vann Woodward, whing-ding fiddle talk and Jim-Crow walk or not, he is the spitting image of the old Life and Casualty Insurance man (or maybe it was Tennessee Life and Casualty or the Industrial Benefit man), whose Willys-Knight you used to snag as if it were a gas-driven L&N switch engine. Anyway, anytime anybody from downhome sees you with either one of them and cocks an ear, popping or cutting his eyes (mostly without changing expression) and waits for you to answer whose is this one and what kind and whose that one, you can say: Filling Station Red. But from Kentucky this time, remembering the smell of the Texaco gas pumps and the inner-tube patching, remembering the free air hose and the old wooden grease rack with the galvanized oil tub, and also remembering the football games on the Atwater Kent radio.

Or in the case of Woodward you can say: Tennessee Life; but from somewhere out in Arkansas this time, remembering how easy it used to be to hobo on dirt-road switch engines, what with spare tires on the back like life preservers—and how easy it was also because he mostly pretended not to see you, and if nobody in the neighborhood spotted you he wouldn't say what he always said until he was ready to pick up speed because he was coming to where the macadam began. And of course you also remember how much fun it also was mocking him in your best whicker-bill twang-nosed throat-locked soda-cracker voice as he pulled on away and out of earshot, you and whoever was with you that particular day saying not, "All right now y'all scat off there now" but: "Say now by Gyard, git the hell and skedaddle offen that durn tyar dang bust you little possums. Dang bust you little possums. Dang bust you little possums. Dang bust you little possums." Which really what old man Lee G. Heatherton from the grocery store always used to say when you snagged the back of the delivery wagon.

You can say that's all right about whing-ding guitars

and Jim-Crow fiddles this time because this one turned out to be the kind who at a time when most students of life in the United States seem to think that cultural assimilation should be measured in terms of Reading Test scores, can say: "The ironic thing about these two great hyphenate minorities, the Southern Americans and the Negro Americans, confronting each other on their native soil for three and a half centuries, is the degree to which they have shaped each other's destiny, determined each other's isolation, shared and molded a common culture. It is in fact impossible to imagine the one without the other and quite futile" —he might, for the benefit of not a few social-science–oriented New York intellectuals, have said "perverse"—"to try"; who in the very same article has written in part: "Two thirds of all the Negroes now living in the North and West were born and raised in the South. They constitute a tremendous Southern impact on the North. Within a few years many of our largest non-Southern cities will be predominantly Negro in population. The North in fact is confronted with a Southern invasion vaster by far than the one General Lee threatened. Under the skin the new invaders are Southern too, even to the second and third generation of them . . . if they can preserve their Southern heritage of endurance, courage and grace under pressure, their country will be better for it. . . ."

You can say: It is C. Vann Woodward, not Beard, Morrison, Commager, Nevins, nor even Aptheker and certainly not Genovese (nor, alas, John Hope Franklin either, though he has other glories) who so far as I know has made a special point of saying and reiterating: "I am

prepared to maintain . . . that so far as culture is concerned, all Americans are part-Negro. Some are more
so than others, of course, but the essential qualification
is not color or race." Not to mention also making a point
to add: "When I say all Americans, unlike Crèvecœur,
I include Afro-Americans. THEY ARE PART NEGRO,
BUT ONLY PART." Nor is the "only" a slur on the
African part—nor is he likely to hold much brief for
those who suggest that the white part of the so-called
half-breed and mulatto is the part that spoils things. No,
the point he makes is that "Negroes are not white people
disguised beneath dark skins and Caucasians are not
black people beneath white skins. . . ."

Not that there aren't other Woodward formulations
that you find somewhat, well, questionable: For instance,
in the very same magazine article in which he defines
downhome Negroes as quintessentially Southern he suddenly gets going on the so-called Negro Middle Class and
turns into a social-welfare polemicist right before your
scandalized eyes. Saying such completely un-Southern
things as, "While the small, mobile, trained middle class
has been moving up, the great mass of Negro workers
has been stagnating or, relative to white workers, losing
ground." Jolly good Big Daddy Moynihan nonviolent
war on poverty jive. But would C. Vann Woodward the
historian draw the same comprehensive inference from
a statement to the effect that the great mass of American
colonists were not moving up at a rate equal to that of
the small mobile trained class that included Thomas
Jefferson, George Washington, and James Madison?
Isn't that small trained elite precisely the class that keeps

the historians in business? Or is Woodward going to give up biography at its age-old literary best for statistics at its politically opportunistic worst? You doubt it. As well you should, for was it not Woodward himself who called upon the historian to abandon false analogies with the natural sciences?

Nor do you feel that fellow Southerner Woodward, as highly as you mostly recommend him, has given proper attention to the question of Negroes and Immigrants. Not that he has ignored the subject. He has some significant things to say about Immigration as such. But when he describes U.S. Negroes as "unneeded and unwanted" he is, to your exasperation, being as soft on the implications of white European immigration as any white supremacist you ever saw in your life. And besides, you have every reason to believe that Woodward, the very embodiment of Southern memory, knows that the Civil War was fought precisely because Negroes were the most wanted laborers in the history of Western civilization, and that he also knows therefore that just as Africans had been trained and conditioned to plantation work they no doubt would have been retrained also to fulfill the requirements of late nineteenth- and early twentieth-century industrialization, but for the influx of white immigrants on preferential quotas. What the hell was Booker T. Washington so concerned about in that Atlanta Compromise speech if not what the immigration of hungry white Europeans would do to the black freedmen? What if not white European immigrant labor was he talking to white Americans about when he not only advised but implored them to "Let down your bucket where you are"?

When Woodward permits himself to say that Negroes were unneeded and unwanted he is, to put it mildly, indulging in polemical abstraction. On the other hand, to point out that white Europeans were permitted to come over here and take jobs which in any other country would have gone first to native-born citizens is to state a historical fact of crucial significance to the present state of the nation's health.

For all that, however, it is C. Vann Woodward (the old life-insurance collector who used to stand in the front yard with one Stacey Adamsed foot propped on the second step scribbling in the policy book) you think about as often as any other historian when you think about new perspectives for American experience. For not only was it the old neatly dressed soft-voiced and not unkindly policeman from Emory in Atlanta, not some Ivy League liberal, who places the Reconstruction sell-out in the context of a national racism geared to imperialism, it is this same downhome white fellow who wrote: "National myths, American myths have proved far more sacrosanct and inviolate than Southern myths. Millions of European immigrants of diverse cultural backgrounds have sought and found identity in them. . . . European ethnic groups with traditions far more ancient and distinctive than those of the South have eagerly divested themselves of their cultural heritage in order to conform."

It was also this same downhome-raised historian who,

with a discernment conspicuously missing in even the best northern historians and reporters, wrote: "The separatists and nationalists have had their native American leaders. But I am more impressed with the association of extremist doctrines of separatism with Caribbean and West Indian leaders and origins going back to Edward W. Blyden of St. Thomas, who swept the South in the nineties, and other worthies including Marcus Garvey of Jamaica and all their mystique of just how black you had to be to be a Negro." On the other hand most northern reporters seem to cling to the old assumption that all Negroes are the same—or should be.

One specific reason for coming to Yale this time is to get his downhome reaction to all of the up-north cocktail-party glibness about the alleged historical differences and natural antagonisms between the descendants of the so-called field Negroes and house Negroes. Because a few misguided TV outspokesmen and consequently a number of white northern journalists are by way of propagating another one of those Elkins type theories of black experience that, to paraphrase Woodward himself, almost make you "despair of history as a path to wisdom."

You have come to this veritable citadel of Yankeedom to see if it is possible to share with him and with Robert Penn Warren something which both he and Robert Penn Warren have claimed as an essential part of the heritage of all post-Confederate downhome folks, "black and white": that *instinctive fear—that the massiveness of experience, the concreteness of life will be violated: the fear of abstraction.*

22

So you sit there in his Sterling Library office looking at him looking almost exactly like the old life and casualty man of your Mobile, Alabama, boyhood, looking precisely as if while you were growing up to go to Mobile County Training School and Tuskegee and so on, he had collected enough policy money to go on off to Emory in Atlanta and then to Columbia and Oxford. This time your response to the whicker-bill otherness of his Arkansas bearing and manner is to remember a scene between Joanna Burden and Joe Christmas in *Light in August*, a scene you have been playing your own changes on ever since you first read it and discussed it with Jug Hamilton at Tuskegee thirty years ago: *Kneel*, you look at him thinking, *I don't ask it. Kneel. Not to me. Not to God. Not to me for forgiveness. Not before God in repentance, which is what Miss Joanna, the liberal do-gooder, who was pregnant, wanted. Not for your grandfathers and the plantations. Not for your father's generation and the Klan. To the facts of life. It is not me that asks it. Remember that. All I ask is that you respect the massiveness of experience, the concreteness of Southern life. All I ask is that you remember what you really know, not what some goddam Yankee polemicist expects all crackers to feel. Man, just consider this: Even old Ulrich B. Phillips (whom shit on) comes closer to the texture of life in bondage as described by my grandparents and yours too than all that Sambo Elkins jive you once gave such a generous blurb to.*

And his response to your question about slave categories is the one you had every reason to expect from a man who has no excuse for not knowing exactly where the old plantations were, where the big houses (some of which were not very big at all) were, where the slave quarters (which were far from always being compounds) were; a man who didn't have to go to Emory and certainly not to Columbia and Oxford to find out who worked precisely where and for how many hours a day and what the daily menu as well as the inventory of the commissary was; a man who like William Faulkner not only knows who owned whose grandparents but also, as little as it is mentioned outside Faulkner, whose blood brothers and sisters and cousins are whose.

"I remember *some* of them from my childhood," he says as unhurriedly as a cracker-barrel stick whittler, "and as you know this goes back some sixty years, when there were quite a few still around." He pauses, whittling. Then: "Yes, my father had dealings with them. We never thought of them like that." Then whittles his metaphorical stick on into an account of the House Slave/Field Slave Dialectic as it is currently being expounded, "by one of my colleagues, a Negro, here at Yale," treating each detail as if it had the challenging insightfulness of Max Weber or Thorstein Veblen. Then he whittles (or cleans and stuffs his metaphorical pipe some more) and adds: "He is quite taken with it. But I have serious doubts about its validity."

It is not a very long visit. There is not really enough stick-whittling time to get into some of the other questions you had in mind, questions, for instance, about whether slaveowners regarded the word "Negro" as being more opprobrious than the word "black," a word whose overwhelming connotations of the negative even the terrifying (the unknown, the mysterious, and death itself—being, incidentally, a universal color of mourning) are by no means limited to references to African-derived Americans. After all, what is largely at issue in the current Afro-Negro-Black controversy over what African-derived Americans should now be called is the white master's usage. As for yourself, you grew up under the impression that white people felt that "Negro" (but not "negress," which is another story like "jewess") was not only a far more respectable term than "black," which always smacked of cargoes, but was actually too dignified to be pronounced correctly—or to be capitalized. It took years of civil-rights protest to get certain national publications to capitalize the word Negro.

Meanwhile, every comment he has made on what you do have time to talk about will stand up very well indeed in all of the best barbershops you have ever known. So *him too. Because if somebody who may be a brownskin Yale student, a brownskin Yale professor, or even a brownskin Yale waiter happens to see you standing there shaking hands and hears the barnyard fiddles in his voice, and just by looking once and a half asks if he is a pretty good one: "Whose is this one? who's vouching this time?" you can smile back nodding without nodding with your eyes saying yes, one of mine, so to speak, me. Yes, better than pretty good, one of the very best around and getting better all the time—and without anybody really checking on him yet. But don't take my word. Check him out for yourself. Read what he writes. Nor is it necessary to be-*

gin with The Strange Career of Jim Crow. *Either* Tom Watson, Agrarian Rebel, The Origins of the New South *or* The Burden of Southern History *will do just fine.*

You sit in Silliman College, Yale, chatting with Robert Penn Warren, poet, novelist, critic, and coauthor of first-rate textbooks for American College English. But what you keep thinking about is the old Telegraph Road which runs (or rather as you remember it used to run) north out of Mobile from St. Joseph Street crossing the Three Mile Creek turn bridge by a cluster of booms, sawmills, and planer mills and going upgrade by Joe Kentz's store past Greer's Hill to Plateau; then crossing the old Magazine Point streetcar line by the Red Brick Drugstore and the white folks' baseball diamond; going to Chickasaw and the shipyards. Because every time you see Robert Penn Warren, whom you have encountered casually and cordially over the past several years and whose nickname is in fact Red as it damn well should be, you remember somebody else named Red: Telegraph Road Red.

So you think: Telegraph Red. Filling Station Red. But not the one who went on to maybe Alabama Poly or Alabama Crimson Tide and maybe the Rose Bowl and afterwards on to cowboy pictures—or maybe came back with his big crimson "A" sweater with the triple sleeve stripes and had his own superservice station and then a chain of them and then became maybe sheriff or maybe commissioner of something. The spitting image

*yes; but a book-reading Filling Station Red from Guth-
rie, Kentucky, who went on to Vanderbilt and California
and Yale and the Oxford of Rhodes Scholars; a book-
reading, book-writing Telegraph Red, some of whose best
stories create an atmosphere which almost always goes
with memories of pale-face dinner-jacket saxophones and
whiskey ruddy trombones tailgating stars falling on
downtown Mobile, Alabama, department stores, stars
trailing an aroma of peanut and popcorn vendors and
five-and-dime perfume counters and sporting-goods
leather; twilight neon stars hovering above Mobile,
Alabama, Coca-Cola fountains (for white people only),
especially people whose friends and associates may have
been Jerry Calhoun and Sue Murdock and some of the
Boss's entourage in* All the King's Men. *But perhaps
most of all the rainbow of stars falling around Slim
Sarrett browsing in Hammel's book corner with a Clark
Gable foreign correspondent's raincoat over his shoulders, and naturally these are the same ones above the
Mobile Press Register Building, where inky-fingered Jack
Burden sits sipping sour mash and typing after-hours
poetry.*

Of course you don't say meanwhile it was really old
then cherub plump Louis Armstrong who could really
make stars fall like confetti—not in the ballroom of the
Battle House of those days to be sure but in Gomez
Auditorium out on Davis Avenue. You don't say only old
Louie could really make all rivers lazy and make it cozy
and cuddly time Down South all over the world. Nor
do you say meanwhile we had not only taken over as our
very own old Hoagy Carmichael's ever so ofay "Stardust"

but had also made it the brownskin dress-parade anthem that went with midnight tinsel much the same as the sound of James Weldon and J. Rosamond Johnson's "Lift Every Voice" used to go with the sepia-tinted pictures of Negro Builders and Heroes on the wall of the old coal stove plus mucilage-scented library at Mobile County Training School. You don't say anything at all about that. But you will always remember the pulsing, guitar-sweetened beat of Victory Dance music, celebrating the MCTS Whippets (and later Tuskegee Golden Tigers) in mufti. *Because there was always a dance afterwards, no matter what kind of contest. Success means being dressed to the nines with stone fox on your arm. As in the balls in* War and Peace, *for instance. But Tolstoy had no Satchmo to sprinkle that kind of stardust in the Russian sour mash. Not that the Russians were ever short on great musicians (whose music sometimes sounds like the very best of the old spirituals). But they didn't sprinkle that kind of stardust; and they didn't play and sing "Chinatown my Chinatown" and "I'm Confessing" and "I Surrender Dear" and "Wrap Your Troubles in Dreams," not like that.*

You don't say Telegraph Red but you think: *Filling Station Red become triple-threat man of letters, who knows what makes a poem or a story tick exactly like old Telegraph Red the master mechanic—who never saw an engine he couldn't tune to purr like a sewing machine. Who used to come blasting by road-testing somebody's motorcycle, used to go hop-skipping somebody's motorboat up and down the Mobile River between Three Mile Creek and the Chickasabogue, old*

Baling Wire Red who also used to come rattling over in a Tailspin Tommy biplane and then circle back up to Chickasaw barnstorming between the AT&N and Bay Poplar.

Of course you don't say anything about road-testing and sour-mash tasting as such. But you do mention a very special old place long familiar to both of you, a book-reader's place called the world of William Faulkner. Then you say: "By the way I brought along a kind of jackleg poem for you, a kind of bootleg poem, if you know what I mean, some jackleg bootleg poetry about that world as now viewed from Lenox Terrace" (thinking also: A kind of shade tree T. S. Eliot poem, a kind of baling wire Ezra Pound Canto, a kind of tin-lizzy "Occasional" after Auden).

Then as you read it as a vamp of blues-idiom piano riffs, a vamp of railroad-guitar riffs, he listens, ear cocked as if with the timing light in one hand and the screwdriver in the other, as if poke-checking the firing order, as if checking and adjusting the carburetor. You read on, thinking: Keep that sour-assed mash moving, horse. Downhome boys got to do better than just hang in there, got to do even better than hang in there together. Maybe downhome boys got to be the ones to point out that if everybody in the nation was just brimming with love for mankind it still wouldn't be enough to circumvent man's fate.

At one point you also say: "One of the things I've been meaning to ask about is the old Fugitive Poets of Nashville. I mean about the origin of the name." And the account he gives is of course literary history of the first order. And the "fugitive" metaphor is valid as far as it goes. But the thing is that so far as you are concerned it didn't really go very far. Not when your idea of the fugitive as ancestral hero is derived from the runaway slave. Not when you remember some of the almost blues-idiom type changes old Faulkner was able to play on the theme of the black runaway, runagate and even renegade in such stories as "Red Leaves," "Was" and "The Bear." Not when you remember Cue in Stephen Vincent Benét's story called "Freedom's a Hard Bought Thing." Putting the young Allen Tate, the young Donald Davidson, and cavalier old John Crowe Ransom in the same base-running, ground-gaining, broken-field razzle-dazzle league with Frederick Douglass and Harriet Tubman was like trying to bootleg George Plimpton into the same lineup with Willie Mays, O. J. Simpson, and Oscar Robertson—as a regular! But you don't say paper fugitives; you ask where the white Southern fugitives of Nashville imagined themselves fleeing to. And it turns out that they were fleeing not so much to as from. " 'We flee,' I think it went," he says remembering, " 'many things.' Let's see, 'but nothing so much,' yes nothing—we can look this up—'nothing so much as the old South, the old Brahmins. . . .' " He goes on remembering and recounting, and it turns out that the fugitives actually fled mostly into the homes of certain very special people in Nashville. He recalls that in addition to the stimulation and encouragement of a few of the instructors at Vanderbilt there were several Jewish businessmen of literary taste in whose homes the white make-believe fugitives found a European atmosphere of arts and letters and even further encouragement and patronage. He mentions names like the Starr brothers, Frank Hirsch; and as he talks your mind leaps forward to the old *Southern Review*, the old *Sewanee Review* and Ransom's old *Kenyon Review* which you used to read at Tuskegee and used to wonder why they also carried some of the same Jewish writers who wrote for such Eastern liberal and left-wing magazines as *Partisan Review, Nation, New Republic*. But you don't go into that either. But you think: *"Midrash." Maybe Stanley Edgar Hyman could have claimed that certain WASPS were sneaking the Talmudic Scholar's Midrash back in there and calling it the New Criticism! The Americanization of the Midrash. But then old Stanley whose Midrashes are geared to the dynamics of a WASP named Kenneth Burke says: "You don't have to be Jewish . . ."*

You don't ask Warren any point-blank questions about the sociopolitical folklore of the white supremacy of Elkins. His current thinking on such lore is, you feel, adequately reflected in the response he makes to your question about the phony issue of house slaves versus field slaves, a response you are delighted to find entirely consistent with your expectations of a downhome white boy whom you respect as a poet, a novelist, and student not only of Southern history and culture but of mankind.

"The wrongs of slavery," he says, "are beyond words, simply beyond words. No question about that, and there is no way that any of it can be excused. No way. It was an awful thing, just awful, a terrible thing. But another thing to remember, and now this you always have to remember. Always. And of course this is the horror

of it, too: that it was also a human thing, institution—
not to say humane—a system made up of human beings,
and in such a system—any system—where what is involved is human beings, every possible, every imaginable,
every *imaginable* combination of human social relationship is likely to exist. *And did exist.* Now that's what it
was."

Could exist, and did exist. As described to a great extent in *Band of Angels*, for instance, and made much
more apparent than in William Styron's *The Confes-
sions of Nat Turner*. But you don't go into that either,
not even to say that most reviewers seemed to have
missed that aspect of it. *That could exist and did exist.*
"As almost always in Faulkner." You do say that, remembering Sutpens Hundred, in *Absalom, Absalom!*;
remembering Uncle Buck and Uncle Buddy in *Go Down
Moses*.

Later on you also think: but then Faulkner, unlike
Thomas Wolfe, the boy from the hill country, had the
memories of a white boy in whose Mississippi Aunt
Hagar was Caroline Barr become Dilsey and Earth
Mother of the Compsons. The literary heritage of William Faulkner included not only books (which big word-
thirsty Thomas Wolfe gulped down as if each was the
last jug of good corn whiskey in the world) but also a
very attentive Mississippi white boy's legacy of outrageous black wit and wisdom from local Uncles Remus
beyond number; and sometimes, as in *Absalom, Absalom!*, he could write out of a background that was so
richly informed by them that it was almost as if he had
even done his book reading like a brownskin downhome

schoolboy doing his homework in the barbershop. Because whatever else *Absalom, Absalom!* is it may also be read in outline as just such a Mississippi white boy's brownskin barbershop version of *Moby Dick*: in which Thomas Sutpen pursues the whiteness of white sons almost precisely as if he were an Appalachian Ahab, only to become inextricably ensnarled with Uncle Remus's Tar Baby disguised this time as a mulatto in Haiti.

Not that William Faulkner didn't have his own confederate hangups. Not that this same William Faulkner couldn't on occasion get himself all worked up as if to mount up for still another Johnny Reb cavalry charge up some long-lost ridge from time to time *"when it is still not yet two o'clock on that July afternoon in 1863, the brigades are in position behind the rail fence, the guns are loaded and ready in the woods and the furled flags are already loosened to break out and Pickett himself with his long oiled ringlets and his hat in one hand probably and his sword in the other looking up the hill waiting for Longstreet to give the word and it's all in the balance."*

But even so it was still this same William Faulkner who probably could have best made even Thomas Wolfe come to appreciate how when you take the "A" train for Harlem you are heading north but also south and home again. Because the voice in which William Faulkner told his downhome yarns may have been ever so much closer to the Scotch-Irish-Gothic-Greek and Latin of Mississippi courthouse square gossip of old man Whicker-bill Charley Comesaw than the railroad-blue-steel-guitar-plus-rawhide-and-patent-leather idiom Uncle

Remus used in the barbershop. Still the best of his yarns not only acknowledge Aunt Hagar and Uncle Remus but also celebrate them as the homefolks most likely not only to endure but to prevail. Nor was his point that the meek shall inherit the earth. His point was that no man could inherit the earth, that the only thing worth inheriting is humanity.

At another point you say: "Speaking of some of the things black and white Southerners share by virtue of growing up in the South, things of cultural or of anthropological significance, things shared in spite of the politics of racism, I guess that briarpatch metaphor behind the title of your piece in *I'll Take My Stand* is something we both got from Uncle Remus in one way or another."

To which he says: "Yes, it was certainly there in the air, all right," and remembers writing the article in England. But you are thinking about the metaphor, not the content of the essay, and you find yourself remembering a Mobile County Training School boy you haven't seen for probably twenty-five or thirty years, a very smooth very dark brown boy whose name was Marion Mayo but who used to call himself Reynard the Fox instead of Brer Rabbit but who not only walked and danced but also ran back punts tip-stepping cute papa cottontail style as if he could wear a pair of patent-leather dress shoes through any briar patch in the world without getting a single scratch on them. (Needless to say there was about as much similarity between your

Remus and the one Joel Chandler Harris wrote about as there is between music as you know it and the way Stephen Foster wrote it. Though sometime old Joel's ear was not bad, not bad at all.)

"Oh no, my pleasure, my pleasure," Warren says, because you are looking at your watch to let him know that you do not intend to take up much more of his time. "No, no, my pleasure."

So the chat continues on into the late Connecticut April afternoon—during which time you make your pet point about Frederick Douglass deserving a place in the national pantheon, and before you get the words out he adds that Douglass's prose also belongs in the nineteenth-century literary canon along with that of Emerson and Thoreau—and then not only do you end up staying for dinner in the Refectory (huddling together as if under a poncho against the shower of media-glib Yankee talk around you. As if before the old Telegraph Road Atwater Kent radio, but talking not about the Crimson Tide or Beatty Feathers of the Tennessee Vols or about books but about a dedicated Tennessee bootlegger named Leroy McAfee and the art of keeping good sour mash moving). You also stay on for an informal discussion by the editor of a national magazine, followed by a party at the headmaster's.

"It will be a pleasure, my pleasure," he says, inviting you to come to see him in Fairfield soon. "It will be my pleasure."

So you come back to New York on the midnight train

35

thinking about Old Telegraph Red. Old Filling Station
Red from Telegraph Road. On whom you have been
filing vouchers for years (even before you pulled down
that A-minus for the one filed at NYU). Ever since back
in college when you came across "The Hamlet of
Thomas Wolfe" and "T. S. Stribling; A Paragraph in the
History of Critical Realism" (also containing an early
assessment of Faulkner as Artist) in Zabel's *Literary
Opinion in America.* But it was with *All the King's Men*
that you really started keeping an eye on him, because
that was where you first ran into that old book-reading
Filling Station Red stuff. In the sensibility of Jack
Burden, the inky-fingered narrator. Then that year at
NYU you finally got into *Night Rider* which you remember only vaguely, and *At Heaven's Gate* which
you enjoyed because you were reading in New York and
there it was again, and there was also Slim Sarrett.

Not Slim Sarrett as such but some of the extracur-
ricular literary stuff he was cut from: *"In the library he
never read a book, except the reserve or reference books
which did not circulate. He checked out books and left.
But one afternoon a week he spent in the periodical
room, reading the current magazines. He never sat down,
but stood before the shelves, his raincoat draped about
his shoulders, the magazine poised in his left hand, the
thumb and forefinger of his right hand holding the
margin of a page, ready to flick it over when he had finished. He read with tremendous rapidity, and without
hesitation in selection, working around the alphabetical
shelves. When he came across an item, especially a*

*poem, which pleased him or irritated him, he walked
over to the desk of a young woman who was in charge,
read the piece to her in his ordinary tone, making no
concession to the sign above the desk. . . ."*

Because that was not only old book-reading, book-writing Telegraph Red himself on his way from, say, Tuscaloosa or Auburn not to murder and flight but to the *Southern Review,* the *Sewanee Review,* and the *Kenyon Review.* It was also Gerald Hamilton at Tuskegee. It was also Ralph Ellison at Tuskegee and it was also you. Because reading it in the Forty-second Street Library you could even smell the floor wax and the furniture polish in the periodicals room of Hollis Burke Frissell. You could hear the Alabama spring rain rattling the drain pipes outside the window. You could even remember exactly how the damp wisteria and freshly-mowed-lawn-scented late April/early May breeze used to feel.

Then there was also the fact that Slim Sarrett was trying to formulate a theory of poetry. That was the sort of thing you were also playing around with even then, which was also when you were reading R. P. Blackmur, Francis Fergusson, Jesse L. Weston, and Kenneth Burke and working on your M.A. thesis about symbols of sterility and fertility in *The Wasteland* and *The Sun Also Rises:* even as you made your regular weekly rounds to hear Dizzy Gillespie, Charlie Parker and young Miles Davis on Fifty-second Street; and to hear Lionel Hampton, Count Basie, and Duke Ellington wherever they were in those good old used-to-be days when you went to such midtown entertainment palaces as the Paramount, the Strand, and Warners' as much for the stage show as for the movie.

All of which was nine years before Warren came to write *Segregation: The Inner Conflict in the South*; it was fourteen before *The Legacy of the Civil War*, and eighteen before *Who Speaks for the Negro?* For the pretty-goodness of which written testimony by you exists.

TWO

GREENSBORO

*Of Hagar-wit and the Nets of
Uncle what-you-may-call-him*

The time en route by railroad is about forty-eight hours when you are lucky enough to make all the connections as scheduled. By Greyhound it is likely to be about thirty. By Whisperjet from La Guardia you can be there in less than four, all told. But this time you go hedge-hopping and whistlestopping by way of Greensboro and Atlanta and Tuskegee. This time also you go on further south from Mobile to New Orleans. Then you head back north by way of Greenville, the legendary levee town of catfish eaters on the ever so hithering-and-thithering Mississlippy Sloppy. Then Lenox Terrace is only two hours northeast from Memphis, Tennessee.

The countryside you see from the limousine going into Greensboro does not remind you nearly so much of the South of Thomas Wolfe, the wild bull of New York literary china shops, as of Jonathan Daniels, of the old Raleigh *News and Observer*, the Jonathan Daniels who wrote the book *A Southerner Discovers the South*, which still stands up as one of the very best personal records of the immediate world you graduated into from college. Indeed, the physical as well as the metaphorical point of departure of *A Southerner Discovers the South* was a commencement ceremony at just such a high school as might have been your own: "The solemn student who had learned all the old phrases that were to his race all too often the parts of an old joke looked like a stupid black satyr, and the girls, whose very skins [which he also describes as taffy- and chocolate-colored] wedded voodoo and pagan, sang around him. But he looked beyond their brief, slim youngness to quotations from Lincoln and Milton, Andrew Jackson and Carlyle, Kipling and Tennyson. 'We go forth,' he said."

"So also I go forth," Daniels continues, "a trifle less confident, a little less certain of Lincoln and Milton as guides, but with an alarm clock set, a tank full of gasoline, a suitcase full of clothes, a suitcase full of books, maps and letters of introduction to the best—the very best—people . . . and into my ears like the South singing rang that whistle voice which took Handel's 'Hallelujah' into the heart of Africa and flung it back again at our South where the north man ultimately met the Negro and built what some have called a civilization. I rode to find it."

He was describing events in North Carolina. But who, after all, if not you at Mobile County Training School in Alabama had recited the following poem from Langston Hughes as the outchorus to your oratorical contest speech:

> *We have tomorrow*
> *Bright before us*
> *Like a flame*
> *yesterday, a night gone thing*
> *a sundown name*

And dawn today
Broad arch above the road we come
We march.

Who if not you and thousands of other bright-eyed "taffy- and chocolate-colored" Southern school boys and girls?—not that you or any schoolmate you ever knew was in the least unmindful of how red the ears of visiting white do-good dignitaries and stand-pat officials alike always turned hearing you put the heart of Africa plus the soul and spirit of Christianity (not unknowingly) into "The Star-Spangled Banner."

And who if not you graduated from Tuskegee four years later as aware of Jonathan Daniels as of Langston Hughes? as aware of the Montgomery *Advertiser* as of the Chicago *Defender*, as aware of Ralph McGill's Atlanta *Constitution* as of the Pittsburgh *Courier?* Who if not you with your clothes and books in your one Gladstone bag caught the bus for your first teaching job over in the Georgia that was still very much the state of Ole Gene Talmadge in spite of Ellis Arnall? Who, having read the *Nation* and the *New Republic* and suchlike including the *New Masses,* was ever more firmly convinced that his own vision was already as far beyond that of W.E.B. as that of Booker T.? Who if not you in that last prewar year of F.D.R.?

So the first thing you and Edwin Yoder, the associate editor (and editorialist even as W. J. Cash, author of *The Mind of the South,* once was) of the Greensboro *Daily News* talk about is young Jo-naythan whom you regard as being as much the son of Chapel Hill at its best as of old Joeseefus, the old Tarheel Editor; young Jo-naythan, who came out of the Chapel Hill of your then Tuskegee-based awareness of things knowing how to use social science without getting lost in pretentious abstractions; young Jo-naythan in his banker's glasses, who wrote as if he were not only as comfortable in seed stores and tobacco warehouses as in libraries and New York literary circles but could also declare that: "we Southerners are of course a mythological people . . . we are in part to blame for our legendary character . . . certainly the land called South is no realm for geographers"; who that long ago could also make the following pronouncement: "But in the South the tyrants and the plutocrats and the poor all need teaching. One of them no more than the others. All are in the warm dark, and whether they like it or not—white man, black man, big man—they are in the dark together. None will ever get to day alone."

He is now old Jo-naythan—not nearly so much in the conventional geriatric sense as in the traditional folk sense that some Southerners become old in your memory and imagination by becoming the fabulously familiar heroes (or villains) of local tall tales during their lifetime. What you actually find yourself thinking is: old *young* Jo-naythan, son of old Joseefus, the old time dimly remembered Tarheel Editor of my young manhood: old *forever young* Jo-naythan, forever young and forever full of piss and vinegar, who wrote such books as A *Southerner Discovers the South* and A *Southerner Discovers New England* as if with the typewriter propped against the dashboard, who got maybe as close to F.D.R. as Jack Burden was to the Boss in *All the King's Men* (up there in the White House with his banker's glasses and his seed- and feed-store facts and figures and his courthouse square yarns which he knew how to spin with exactly the right contemporary Southern mixture of inky-fingered journalistic hipness and immediacy and Chapel Hill grass roots—not without the expected overtones of ante-bellum book learning and phrase turning to be sure).

The only reason you don't make the short trip over to Raleigh to meet and chat with him as Edwin Yoder can easily arrange for you to do is that Daniels, who is no longer editor but now publisher, is not there. He doesn't spend much time at the *News and Observer* any more. Nowadays he is, it seems, most often to be found at Hilton Head, his soft weather retreat off the coast of Savannah. He comes into Raleigh from time to time, but for the past several years he seems to have been spending his time mostly writing books. You remind Yoder that it is not really Jonathan Daniels himself in the flesh that you have come to make personal contact with anyway, but rather (as metaphysical as it might sound), the idea (even more than the specific ideas!) of Jonathan Daniels.

"The Jonathan Daniels fallout, man. Among the younger fellows. You know what I mean? Like yourself."

Still, it would have been nice to meet old Jo-naythan on the hoof at long last and tell him something about what his book meant to you that long ago. And you may or may not have also told him about how on your way

45

forth from college out into the world of that South he
had then so recently described in terms so specifically
similar to the emphasis of certain of your courses in
Social Science and Education, the Greyhound from
Tuskegee had pulled into Columbus, Georgia, too late to
make the connection with the Trailways bus to Blakely
down in Early County, and you had by a chance but
fabulously appropriate encounter met with a young road
musician and had spent the night on a couch in the red-
velvet-draped, tenderloin-gothic, incense-sultry sickroom
of the legendary but then long since bedridden Ma
Rainey.

That would have been determined by Daniels' response to what you most certainly have said about your
conception of the blues as an idiom of experience-con-
frontation, and existential improvisation; as a frame for
definition within which Uncle Remus, an artistic ancestor of Jelly Roll Morton and Louis Armstrong alike, is
the spinner of such yarns and the weaver of such nets
as become meshes to catch the wind, and in which Aunt
Hagar, the earth-dark coziness of whose bosom is the
wellspring of all mother-wit, is the supreme big mamma
of those blue-steel cradles out of which endlessly rock-
ing (and cooling it too) come all "taffy and chocolate"-
colored wayfaring forth-farers.

Nor did they cling to the old promise quite as naively
as some white boys might imagine. On the contrary, it
was most likely to be the bright-eyed white boy himself
(even one as free of the conventional Protestant ethic
rat-race-ism as Young Jo-naythan), who was all too easily

seduced by *Poor Richard's Almanac*, not the children of
Aunt Hagar and Uncle Remus (to whom Po' Richard's
Yankee Doodle pre–Horatio Alger jive about early to
bed, early to rise is likely to sound like some more of old
Marster's cotton-picking bullshit)!

But back to what Aunt Hagar in the old whispering
blues-dive–diva timbre of Ma Rainey actually sang to the
young initiate from Tuskegee: "*Your money can't pay
for nothing in this house, my precious. Not in Mama's
house, darling. Just go on the way you going, sweetheart,
and just be careful.*" (Nor did she, or anybody else, have
to remind you that from junior high school on having
an education was as dangerous as it was precious, that
a brownskin boy with education made white people even
more uneasy than the idea of a man with a concealed
weapon.) "*No, honeypie, Mama knows what you trying
to do, and it takes more than a notion, more than a
notion and every little bit helps. Mama just wants you
to know how proud she is you come to her. Mama Gertrude always did back up her chillun and always will as
long as she's got breath in this old body.*"

Nor did she have to tell you that you were supposed
to strut your stuff for Mama. The way she patted your
shoulder and stroked your arm said that as clearly as
you for one would always remember her saying it on the
stage when you were still a preschool tot on the outskirts
of Mobile, Alabama, and they used to come tail-gating
around on a platform truck advertising for the vaudeville.
She would be wearing a shimmie-she-wabble-spangled
dress and her blues-queen sequined headband and as

each musician moved into the solo spot she would say, "*Yes, darling, yes, sweet Papa brownskin, now strut your brownskin stuff for Mama, Sweet Papa brownskin.*"

All mamas were always saying that to you in one way or another whatever they were talking about: "*Play the little man for Mama, Albert Lee. Just play the little man for mama. That's all right about that old booger man. You just be the little man for Mama. You just be my little Mister Buster Brown man. Mama's little Mister Buster Brown man ain't scared of no booger man and nothing else. Mama's little man ain't scared of nobody and nothing in creation—or tarnation either. Because Mama's little man is Mama's BIG man, just like him daddy that's what him is. That's exactly what him is, betchem bones. Him momom Mitchem Buttchem Bwown. Momoms itchem bittchem Mittchem Buttchem Bwown; betchem tweet bones.*" Then there was that song by Sissle and Blake, "If You've Never Been Vamped by a Brownskin You've Never Been Vamped at All."

As far as you yourself are concerned the connection between Aunt Hagar and Ma Rainey and Mama on the one hand and the Harriet of young Jo-naythan's boyhood is quite obvious. "My first guide," he declares in *A Southerner Discovers the South*, "was Harriet, yellow and wise, who could look all that the conventional Mammy was supposed to be but who possessed knowledge and interests which made childhood under her guiding a dark excitement of endless variety."

But how much connection between that profoundly intimate part of his childhood and your own would he have been prepared to acknowledge? and once that acknowledgment was made, how ready would he have been to see the contrast that you would insist on pointing out? After all, for all their seed-store sense of actuality, those Southern white boys who are lucky enough to have mammies to celebrate are forever getting so totally carried away with narcissistic sentimentality that they create the absolutely astonishing impression that black mammies existed only to love and care for *white* children. So far as every last mammy-oriented white Southerner you ever meet was concerned it was as if their black mammies cared nothing at all for their own children, not to mention their own children's children. Such white Southerners seem to take it for granted that their mammies did not think their own children were as good and as deserving as white children! Well, in all your days of awareness you'd only met a few of Aunt Hagar's children, whether black, brown, or mulatto, who couldn't tell them a thing or two about all that.

Most of the time you just let them go on because they sounded so corny and it was so easy to embarrass them. But sometimes when they kept going on and on, you had to cut in: "O.K., man. I hear you and I heard it before, and maybe I don't know what the hell your good old black-molasses sweet Mammy-madonna told you about little old chicken-butt me but I can tell you a whole lot of things she was telling me about y'all at the same time."

One thing she was always saying for example was: *"Mamma's little man ain't no little old crybaby like no little old white boy always got to have somebody petting*

49

*him every time he got a little scratch on him some-
where. Mamma kissing Mamma's little man because
she just want her some of that sweet old little pretty-
man sugar that's what she kissing and hugging him so
about."*

Then there were the sometimes endlessly reiterated
admonishments, such as: *"Boy, don't you ever let me
catch you going around this house dropping your clothes
and things all over the place and leaving them like you
living in some kind of old pig pen or something, and you
got somebody hired to pick up behind you. You ain't no
little old spoiled white boy, and we ain't no white folks
so lazy we got to have somebody else to help keep our
house clean like folks suppose to. That's old poor white
trash lying around in all that muck and mire because
they can't pay nobody to keep them and their chillun
clean, not us. I'm raising you to keep yourself neat and
clean and looking like somebody think something of
yourself. Myself I just can't sit down till this house is
clean, don't care how tired and wore out I come in. I
can't sleep in no filthy house. Lord it just makes my
flesh crawl to see folks sitting in a dirty house. I just
can't help it. I just can't stand no dirty house. I for one
don't mean to raise no youngun to grow up and work
his wife to death cleaning up after him."*

And sometimes, not so much in reprimand as in
gratuitous warning: *"Mind you manners, my young man.
Ain't no child of mine going to be talking back at no
grown folks like them little old sassy white chillun bristl-
ing and talking back up at their mammas and daddies
like there ain't no God in heaven and no hell in the*

hereafter. Being nice and mannerable to grown folks ain't never done no youngun no harm, and you never can tell when you going to need somebody to put in a good word for you somewhere one of these days. You just remember that, my young man, when you get to feeling mannish; and keep your big talk to yourself when you around grown folks."

To which, when the time came, she was to add: *"Control your nature. Ain't nobody never going to make nothing out of hisself if he let his nature run away with him. Talking about your nature going to your head that's exactly when it's going to your head because that's when you ain't going to know whether you going or coming. Ain't no use in me wasting my time telling you something you ain't going to do so that's why I mean exactly what I say. I ain't said nothing about denying your manful nature. I said control your nature because that's exactly what a real man can do. That's what a woman expects a man to do. That's what a woman loves a man for doing."*

As for what a unanimity of black mammies, Aunt Hagars, and mammas actually said, and signified when the time came to talk about white girls, more often than not it was as if the same voice were speaking through different (but not very different) masks: *"Just remember this, my young mister man, and you can forget it if you want to but I know what I'm talking about because I ain't talking about nothing I read in no book I'm talking about flesh and blood. So I'm going to tell you anyhow my young man and if you don't listen I'm here to tell you someday you'll wish you had. So you can mock my*

*words if you want to but when one of them little old
white gals say something to you I just want you to know
the chance you taking. I raised many a one, and God
knows I know ain't nothing in creation more selfish and
deceitful than some little old spoiled white child snug-
gling up to you for you to tell a lie to cover up something
and will turn right around and lie you in all kinds of
trouble without batting an eye and then come sidling up
expecting you to forgive them. That's the first thing. And
another thing is you ain't nobody's playpretty to be
picked up and thrown away whenever they like. Boy,
do you hear what I say? I know you got sense enough to
know that anybody who ain't going to help you get out
of the trouble they got you into ain't no friend of yours.
I know good and well you got sense enough to know
that, so that's all I got to say about that and you better
remember it the rest of your born days. If you don't and
let them grin your neck into a rope, no better for you."*

(As for what such mammies, mamas, and aunts said
about the so-called Southern belle, obviously they didn't
tell their white boys what they got around to telling you
sooner or later: *A frisky-tail gal is a frisky-tail gal, don't
care how much they pay for her perfume. You see them
white gals sashaying around actin all stuck up and
making out like they just stepped out of a doll house or
somewhere, well I'm here to tell you they ain't no china
dolls, don't care how much powder and rouge they got
on. Who you reckon keeping that dollhouse clean, such
as it is? On top of washing and ironing them clothes and
tying them ribbons and bows. Who you reckon they mamas learned to from, and they mamas's mama? Who*

*you reckon the last one all of them always come to show
themselves to just before they go flouncing off somewhere to make a fool out of another one of them little
old mannish white boys all growed up putting on airs
and calling hisself a gentleman? And don't bit more
know what they doing than the man in the moon. Who
you reckon the one made him learn all them fancy manners he showing off?"*)

When William Faulkner declares as he did in the eulogy
he delivered at her funeral that his black mammy was a
"fount of authority over my conduct and of security for
my physical welfare, and of active and constant affection
and love," and that she was also "an active and constant
precept for decent behavior, from her I learned to tell
the truth, to refrain from waste, to be considerate of the
weak and respectful of age," you don't doubt that he was
deeply moved as he spoke or was moved again every
time he remembered what he said, but being one of black
mammy's taffy- and chocolate-colored boys you could not
only tell him a few things, you could also ask him a hell
of a lot of pretty embarrassing questions, beginning, for
instance, with: "Damn man, if the mammyness of blackness or the blackness of mammyness was so magnificent
and of such crucial significance as you now claim, how
come you let other white folks disrespect and segregate
her like that? How come you didn't put yourself out just
a little bit more to please her? How can fellows like you
be so enthusiastic about her and yet so ambivalent and
hesitant about her brothers and sisters? Man, do you
really think that your reciprocation was adequate? Have

you ever been tempted, if only for a moment, to take some little taffy and chocolate child to your bosom as my Aunt Hagar did to you? I mean, damn, man, the least y'all rich ones could do is set up some Aunt Hagar fellowships something like that Rhodes scholar jive."

But that is old stuff, so old that it is hardly worth a barbershop shrug. Yet in view of all the recent New York drawing-room theoretics about black matriarchs what is passing strange is that none of the big fatheaded Marx-plus–Freud–oriented experts on black identity who are so glib about family structures and filial relationships otherwise have made absolutely nothing of the fact that white boys from the "best" Southern families have not only almost always claimed to have had black mammies but have also invariably depicted them as representing the quintessence of Motherhood! Many white Southerners go around talking about white womanhood or really about white girlhood which is to say belle-hood, but the conception of *Motherhood,* for some reason almost always comes out *black!* And yet not even those Freud-derived New York Jewish writers who are forever and ever complaining about their Yiddisher mamas have even made a second-rate joke or two about this particular characteristic of downhome goy boys.

Nevertheless what a Marx-Freud–oriented piece of Americana for, say, *Commentary* or *Dissent!* what with literary footnotes and psychopolitical cross-references and all. And besides, who knows? Such a piece might help even Norman Mailer to make up his mind as to whether he wants to be a Texan or an Irishman (say, like Big Daddy Pat Moynihan), or maybe he'll settle for being a U.S. Levi Yitzchak of Berdichev after all. But what a piece of Americana somebody like say Norman Podhoretz could make if he decided he didn't like white Southerners anymore or if he could ever figure out which New York Southerners are Compsons and which are Snopeses. Such a piece could also in classical New York Marx Freud baroque style explore the possible connections between the so-called Mafia and the *mamma mia* dimension of the U.S. Italian experience. But seriously you can only wonder what happens to all that fancy Teachers College–plus–Bruno Bettelheim jive about the first few years of childhood being the most crucial, when the topic is the black mammy's relationship to the white child.

It is not, however, primarily for echoes of Aunt Hagar that you listen during your conversations with Edwin Yoder. You expect to pick up some overtones and reverberations, of course. But what you have actually come hoping specifically to hear interwoven with Yoder's own particular seed-store–feed-store plus courthouse square plus Chapel Hill plus Oxford Rhodes scholar sensibility is not so much an Aunt Hagar as an Uncle Remus (or Uncle Remus–derived) dimension of downhome or blues-idiom orientation to the ambiguities of human actuality, an Uncle Remus–derived respect for human complexity, a Brer Rabbit–derived appreciation for human ingenuity.

But you have decided not to ask any point-blank questions about that sort of thing either, this time, not in Greensboro or anywhere else. Not only because (once again) not to have to ask is precisely the point, but also because point-blank answers and acknowledgments seldom tell you enough. Because at bottom the point is not really a matter of how Remus-conscious he is or how much specific credit he is willing to concede but rather how much Remus-type insight he brings to bear upon things as a matter of course.

So you don't ask him if he is one of Uncle Remus's white boys or whether his father or his father's father was one—and besides that is not necessarily the most direct line of inheritance anyway. As far as the dynamics of such inheritance go all you have to do is remember how many white musicians, for instance, have become the children of fabulous Uncle Louis Armstrong without ever fully realizing it because they simply do not know that much about how they came to be the way they are. Sometimes they get it out of the air. After all, the airways are saturated with perhaps even more of Uncle Dipper's flushed-face white sons both legitimate and illegitimate than his short-coupled and sometimes-long-gone-a-wee-bit-further black ones.

Of course you could ask whatever became of all those little wide-eyed spellbound white boys who used to spend so much time sitting at the feet of Uncle Remus. What the hell did they ever do with all those fantastic nets to catch wisdom that he used to weave for them? You could say: "We know all about those who grew up to parlay the rhetoric into political bullshit (and bullshit mostly against black folks at that), but what about the others, the pretty-good ones who like his 'coffee- and taffy-colored' nephews knew that such nets were woven of the eternal verities?"

And incidentally you could also remind him and them of something else: That it is European theory-oriented New York intellectuals, not courthouse-square Southerners who are most likely to mistake the concrete virtues of Uncle Remus (and Aunt Hagar) for the abstract attributes of Rousseau's "noble savage." To the white Southerner who as a little boy sat at his feet (and went fishing, hunting, and on journeys with him) and as a young man served his agricultural and technological apprenticeship under him, Uncle Remus was not only a fundamental symbol of *time-honored authority*, he was also, as they say in New York, A FATHER FIGURE!, whose sense of complexity and whose intellectual sophistication is anything but that of a "noble savage." (Now how about some Oedipus-complex talk in a Hagar-Remus context?)

(Also few aspects of the current conflict over school desegregation strike you as being more ironic than the fact that mass-media commentators and white middle-income Southerners alike now seem totally unaware of the fact that the best-brought-up Southerners have always depicted Aunt Hagar and Uncle Remus to the world as the most expert preschool and elementary-school child psychologists in the history of child development. And that as soon as the poor white Southerner can afford to do so he hires the nearest thing to Uncle Remus and Aunt Hagar he can come by to bring up his children properly! Nor is the irony restricted to the matter of child rearing. As soon as your ambitious poor white Southerner becomes affluent enough to buy a fine house, the very first thing he seems most likely to do is to bring Negroes into the inner circle of his family life. Of course

57

he calls them his servants, or even his house niggers, but everybody knows very well that he has really hired them because they are the experts who can teach him to live in style like the white gentry from which many poor whites have been more completely excluded than most downhome Negroes have ever been.)

Actually, in the case of Edwin Yoder, you are inclined to assume from previous encounters—and from some of his articles—that you can use the fiction of William Faulkner as an Uncle Remus touchstone, or range finder, that all you have to do is allude to some character and situation in one of old Uncle Whicker-Bill's Yoknapatawpha yarns and listen for the Remus overtones in the feedback. But as a matter of fact you are also inclined to assume that you don't even have to do that. Because regardless of the specific nature and degree of his personal contact with the Remus dimension of the Southern experience perhaps the most distinctive feature of Yoder's bearing and presence, clean-cut fair-haired North Carolina boy good looks aside, is the twinkle which always lights up his expression whenever some topic engages him. Indeed, you like to think that it is precisely that Uncle Remus–derived twinkle (which is to say sense of humor and of the absurd—which is to say actuality, the perception thereof, at long range) that could be his best security against the nonsense, terminological and otherwise, that is too typical of so many other newsmen and editorialists these days.

So in point of fact you shouldn't have to use even Faulkner this time. All you should have to do is riff a couple of satchmo-elegant blues choruses on any subject whatsoever and then lay out for a few bars and listen for his jack teagarden rejoinder, as it were. But you go ahead and sound a faulkner chord anyhow. Because when you come down to the fundamentals of what you are really trying to do, you are really only using Uncle Remus himself as a touchstone for—or perhaps rather as a steppingstone to—the point you would like to make about the sad state of journalism these days, what with so many reporters substituting social-science theory and terminology for open-minded observation or just plain old-fashioned human interest, curiosity, and even hard-headed detective-story–type investigation. So what you go ahead and do is you point out how Faulkner, for his part, could use frank speculation and conjecture as literary devices or nets to catch the human content of time and motion: specifically, how by having Quentin Compson and Shreve McCannon talking years later at Harvard make up details about events not actually witnessed by themselves in Mississippi, Faulkner renders the essential truth of the climax of the story of Thomas Sutpen, and of Henry Sutpen and Charles Bon, the ill-fated half-brothers in *Absalom, Absalom!*

The point of course is that so many reporters mistake social-science metaphor for facts these days, without realizing that even the most precise concepts are only nets that cannot hold very much flesh-and-blood experience. Whereas the most pragmatic thing about *poetic* metaphor is that you know very well that your net cannot trap all of the experience in question. Indeed, you often feel that maybe most of it has eluded you. (Hence, such figures of speech as simile, metonymy, synecdoche, hyperbole, irony, and so on.) You readily concede that formulations generalized from scientific-research findings may be nets with a closer weave, still not only do they remain nets, but at best they trap even smaller areas of experience than literary configurations, expressly because they are necessarily in a narrower weave. As with what Kenneth Burke calls "trained incapacity," scientific insight may be more sharply focused but its field of vision is likely to be correspondingly more limited.

At one juncture, speaking of terminology as preconception you also say: "I have a thing about the way journalists misuse the word 'ghetto.' Naturally, I don't want to become a goddam nut about it; but, man, the chickenshit way they now use it, the word itself is equivalent to predefinition and prejudice. It equals prejudging, preinterpreting, preevaluating conduct from location, and not only conduct but character, personality. In other words, as I see it, inherent in the word itself is a very strong danger of overinterpreting both behavior and personality in terms of environment. You know what I mean? It's like saying, I know who you are and what you are going to do and why, because I know where you come from. Which is a lot of crap. Well, what I'm suggesting is that such journalists work from an inadequate grammar of motives. You know Kenneth Burke's work? His five key terms of dramatism: scene, act, agent, agency, and purpose? Well, what I mean is when they use 'ghetto' the way they do they are really trying to explain all action and purpose from scene alone—which just can't be done, especially when all you think you need to know about circumstance is a bunch of goddam statistics, computed to substantiate some half-assed theory."

It so happens that it is also to *Absalom, Absalom!* that Yoder has already referred in his essay "W. J. Cash After a Quarter Century" to point out that Southern literature "where one encounters directly the fetishes of family, physical place, and tradition," provides the best approach to the "mystical" side of the mind of the South. Moreover, it is in the very same allusion that he complains that communication of the Southern experience (even in such "bloody and tortured Iliads" as Faulkner's) is difficult in a highly commercialized and mobile society that has replaced ties of blood and household with "abstractions of a fairly impersonal sort."

There is then, little doubt that Yoder shares your misgivings about conclusion-jumping no less than do Robert Penn Warren and C. Vann Woodward; and as the conversation continues you become more and more impishly amused at your not altogether frivolous notion that his twinkle may be the reflection of a sense of humor inherited from an Uncle Remus–type sense of human complexity. Not that you are in the least unappreciative of the fact that some pretty good old yarns are also derived from the old Anglo-Saxon cracker-barrel pubs and coffeehouses. There is, also and also and also, you hasten to concede, his inheritance from Chaucer and Shakespeare, to name only two of an endless number. *But still and all you are prepared not only to suggest but also to insist that the downhome cracker barrel can always do with some of Uncle Remus's very special old fireside insights into the nature of the briar patch to temper some of that ever so easy and self-indulgent Confederate sentimentality that is forever at odds with what Warren calls "the fear of abstraction."*

Nevertheless you don't ask the all too obvious question —how far Edwin Yoder or any other white Southerner is prepared to go on the question of Southern heritage and identity, on the matter, that is to say, of the consequences of all those black bosoms and hearthstone uncles. Because once again, and again and again, the point is not to ask point-blank but to discover in due course. Because furthermore, in addition to any personal and local (which is to say, political) hangups that may inhibit a direct response there is also the likelihood that many are honestly unaware of the possibility that some of their whitest ancestors may have had black ancestors of one kind or another. That possibility after all is perhaps the source of at least as much obfuscation as anything else. Nor is such obfuscation limited to white Southerners.

Yet even as they concede, as not a few so readily do, that you for your part may be one of William Faulkner's brownskin book-reading sons you immediately and inevitably become by physical as well as logical extension not only one of William Faulkner's black mammy's brownskin grandsons, but in consequence also the bright-eyed ever so Buster-Brown yard-nephew of Uncles Remus (or Bud or Doc or Mose or Ned), both numberless and timeless.

Indubitably. And in addition to being the most ex-

pert of all downhome handymen and ex-riverboat roustabouts, were not such uncles (whether of the fireside or
barbershop variety) also among other things the most
town-hip as well as roadwise of any chauffeur who ever
Cadillacked an avenue; the most patent-leather–smooth
of all old pro butlers and maître d's, the most déjà-vu
confidential of all transcontinental Pullman porters, the
most omniflexible and cosmopolitan of all transoceanic
merchant seamen, as much at home in Joseph Conrad's
Singapore as in Boston and Charleston and San Francisco? Indubitably.

So you could also always say this too: *Hey look man,
the same old ever-so-easily-forgotten-to-be-partially-re-
membered Remus, who in the etceteralogical wisdom
of his incomparable uncleness used to spin for you and
all wide-eyed tell-me-tale taddy white boys such weather-
worthy yarns as make such nets as can hold what is
seizable of winds plus somewhat comprehensible of
human motivation is not only the selfsame old uncle
copper-coin–colored Bud-Doc-Mose-Ned who used to
hand-take me fishing and crabbing on Three Mile Creek,
who built me toy fair castles along rockabye rivers but
is also the same who in the fullness of his fablehood and
in the intrinsicality of his honorificity has taught me the
sociologistics of nightclub entertainers and road musicians, the psychologistics of skin-game survivors and the
vernacularities of calculus and trigonometry among other
unmentionable unmentionables during all my steel-blue
times in rook joints and jook joints, for all the A-B-C
days I spent in book joints.*

Indeed you could also point out that so far as you

63

personally were concerned it was Uncle Bud-Doc-Mose-Ned-Remus, not Henry James, who first said: *"Boy, keep your eyes and ears open. Boy, try to be one on whom nothing is lost."*

But you don't say any of that either. Nor do you point out that it was not Magnolia Moonshine but such uncles that most likely had most often fubbed the girandoles of the most opulent post-bellum mansions of the most fortunate of fair-haired downhome white boys. Nor do you describe him as the best of all emperors of back-porch ice cream or suggest that disguised as Chick Webb or Cozy Cole or Sonny Greer or Jo Jones or Big Sid Catlett with a wooden spoon he gouged out the eyes of the crocodiles and beat the monkeys on the behind, in the Savoy ballroom.

What you do say are words to the following effect about what you insist are terminological preconceptions: Another name for the misapplication of the word "ghetto" by cliché-conditioned journalists is the Scenic Fallacy—which is also of a piece with several other commonly accepted assumptions underlying currently popular misrepresentations of black experience. There is the Sambo Fallacy, for instance, growing out of the contention that the experience of slavery and oppression has reduced U.S. Negroes to a subspecies consisting of a passel of emasculated, shuffling, driveling, head-scratching darkies. There is also the Minority-Group Psyche Fallacy which functions no doubt to reassure race-war–oriented white cowards that U.S. Negroes have a built-in sense of inferiority because they represent only one-tenth [sic!] of the population. And then there is the Self-Image Fallacy that permits white oneupmen to interpret all black American artwork as a reflection of low self-esteem.

The giveaway on the Sambo Fallacy is the all too obvious fact that white Americans have long been mostly terrified by the tales of uptown violence allegedly committed by downtown Sambos. How can all of the police-documented violence possibly issue from personality structures that are emasculated? The "political" behavior of employees vis-à-vis their supervisors just simply cannot be equated with their total makeup. (*Why is nothing ever made of the fact that to be Afro-American is to be derived at least in part from a mask-wearing tradition?*)

What exposes the Minority Psyche Fallacy is the fact that if you live in a black community the world·looks black. You can't be ignorant of the world at large and overimpressed by it at the same time, and the same holds for the statistics of demography: You can't be ignorant of fractions and percentages and oppressed by your awareness of their significance at the same time. As for the self-image as self-rejection ploy, what could be more patently ridiculous than the assumption that the so-called average student's mastery of the tools of communication are such that he can express exactly what he sees and feels? Any competent language teacher knows better than that, and any art teacher knows that the language of art is not to be confused with conventional methods of communication. On the other hand, how well-informed are social scientists on what art communicates in its own terms as artistic expression? Yet, what nobody ever suggests is that black people, whether pupils or spokesmen, may misrepresent themselves, whether through incompetence or by design, or that they use a language which is beyond conventional interpretation. Whatever happened to the fact that some people speak foreign languages? Some, it must be remembered, even speak private languages.

(Later you realize that you forgot to point out to Yoder that the very use of the word "ghetto" is in itself a part of an insidious process of ghettoization, as attitudes and the course of events in Harlem during the past several years make only too obvious. And yet such is also the nature of linguistic vulgarization involved that even now the word ghetto is beginning to take on some less pejorative connotations: Hey look, Murray, it's only natural that each man sees the world from his own ghetto, McGeorge Bundy sees it from his, Senator Jake Javits sees it from his, Fulbright sees it from his, so naturally Dr. Kenneth P. Clark sees it from his just like the same thing goes for Rockefeller.

And still later there was also this:

> *Gimme a good ole ghetto man*
> *Say now goo(h)ood oho ghe-he-tow man*
> *Cool in the summer*
> *Mellow in the fall*
> *Warm me in the winter*
> *Hmn springtime, Lordy Lord . . .*

Except for lunch at a restaurant down the street, a sightseeing stroll around downtown Greensboro, and brief visits to A&T College and to Bennett College, neither of which you have seen since the time you made a trip there for a conference when you were an undergraduate at Tuskegee, you spend all of your too brief North Carolina stopoff in the editorial rooms of the *Daily News.*

Then back at the airport waiting for the flight to Atlanta you amuse yourself by thinking up ways to vouch for the indispensable smattering of the black mammy-wit you've always discerned behind Jonathan Daniels' Chapel Hill–polished banker's glasses and the smidgen of old Uncle Ned in Edwin Yoder's Oxford–cracker-barrel twinkle as against Thomas Wolfe's starry-eyed, box-ankled, sweaty-palmed, drooly-lipped eagerness to devour the whole earth raw.

But then you had already decided years ago that the thing about Thomas Wolfe is that he never found out that the whiteness of white skin is only skin deep and that the rest is mostly human nature and tradition or conditioned conduct. But alas, poor Thomas Wolfe seemed to think that the whiteness of dixie white skins was whale deep and not unlike Faulkner's demonic Thomas Sutpen, he chased the whiteness of whiteness like *yes* a hillbilly Ahab all his life. But he chased it on a treadmill, mistaking his mirror for time and the river, dashing off books like long-winded notes to be left in bottles in the Ocean Sea, books which read for the most part as if they were not so much written as shouted. Maybe he was shouting for help. Maybe for just such help as good old Aunt Hagar and wonderful old Uncle Remus might have given but for the asking.

THREE

ATLANTA

Scoring Position, Peachtree Street

One very specific objective of the trip back this time is to chat with a few writers and intellectuals like Edwin Yoder going about their routine everyday business in their natural Carolina, Georgia, Alabama, Louisiana, Mississippi, and maybe Tennessee habitat. Not that you've undertaken it on your own. Maybe somebody should, but you like it better the way it is. Because this way it is not you who asks anything of them. It is the editor of Harper's Magazine. *It is Willie Morris, who is himself one of them. It is Willie Morris from Yazoo City, Mississippi. It is Willie Morris who came north by way of Texas and Oxford looking for home and so is perhaps somewhat closer in some ways to the black renegades, the old underground runagates, than to the paper fugitives of Nashville, however much he may admire their high esthetic standards.*

All you did was get started on your line about Ralph McGill and Jonathan Daniels being perhaps the true ancestral figures of some of the better young Southern newspapermen today. That was back several years ago while McGill was still alive; and what Willie Morris had said then was, "And Hodding Carter." Then he had said, "Well, look, why don't you go down at our expense and see what kind of piece you can do about it?" Then later when Harper's Going Home in America *series was in the planning stage: "Why don't you make a circle down and back spending a little time visiting with some of them. We'll make the contacts with the ones you don't know already. There's also Marshall Frady and Pat Watters and Joe Cumming and Jack Nelson, in Atlanta. I think you'll find they're all pretty good old boys, and let's see, John Corry will call Ray Jenkins in Montgomery. I know young Hodding and Dave Halberstam knows them. You've met Walker Percy. Maybe he can set you up with Shelby Foote in Memphis. Why don't you go and come on back and see what you can do on that."*

So it is Willie Morris (for all his leftover white Southern schoolboy enthusiasm for Thomas Wolfe) and the point is precisely that you yourself do not have to ask it. Because so far as that goes the main thing is not how free you yourself are to make such requests (though that is not to be dismissed) but rather how free they are to volunteer that which should be as significant to them as to you in the first place.

"I think you ought to take time out and see what you can come up with. You'll probably get yourself a book out of it."

He then went on to reiterate that it didn't have to be anything at all like the usual news report. So you've decided to take the literary options. But still and all if you could bring it off, the ever so newsworthy political implications would be obvious enough; and after all doesn't anything that any black, brown, or beige person says in the United States have the most immediate political implications? No strain for that. But the overall statement would be literary—as literary, which is to say as much of a metaphorical net, as you could make it. What with everybody going in for the personal position paper these days, maybe you could vamp your way into a few of your own

*riffs on the old meandertale you think you can hear over-
tones of in "Cottontail," for instance, to mention only
one of a thousand and one ambivalent fox-trots, in the
Ellington repertory alone.*

In all events you have picked up the Harper's Magazine *advance against expenses and are en route south,
this time not as a reporter as such and even less as an
ultra gung-ho black black spokesman but rather as a
Remus-derived, book-oriented downhome boy (now
middle-aged) with the sort of alabama buster brown–hip
(you hope) curiosity "that implies impression that knits
knowledge that finds the nameform that whets the wits
that convey contacts that sweeten sensation that drives
desire that adheres to attachment that dogs death that
bitches birth that entails the ensuance of existentiality."
If you could get enough of all that together you were
pretty certain that all of the required polemics would also
be there as a matter of course.*

As the flight moves along the taxiway to the Atlanta
terminal in the twilight you feel some old familiar
twinges of red alertness in that part of you that will
never get used to not being welcome. But it is not the
old downhome radar that clicks on first this time. It is
the old midtown Manhattan subterfuge detector. Because
what you are going to find out shortly now is whether
the greatly improved Atlanta you have been hearing and
reading so much about has improved only up to the

point at which midtown Manhattan was back in the old not so long ago days when you first started making trips up the country—a point beyond which, incidentally, as no apartment hunter will dispute, midtown Manhattan has not gone very far as of today.

So preparatory to everything else you check with you-know-precisely-which-good-old-you-know-who: "Hey man, I'm stopping off here to see some newspaper people tomorrow and maybe the next day. Can you recommend a good downtown hotel?" (*Which is buster brown for:* "*Hey man, can you vouch for what these goddam old Alana peckerwoods been doing since I was through here last time?*") You don't say price is no sweat because he has already checked out your luggage, your fly tailoring, your big-league cameras, because he does that on super-high-speed ektachrome, 160 at f stop 16, shutter speed 1/1000.

He nods toward the battery of "Instant Hotel Reservations" telephones across from the luggage-claim point.

"Take your pick."

Then he adds: "The limousine makes all the rounds—or if you want a taxi."

You tip him and he smiles an old Joe Louis unsmile and winks an old johnny hodges sir cedric hardwick–cool things-aint-what-they-used-to-be unwink.

It only takes an instant as advertised. *But the sudden activation of the radar has changed your mood. So you ride in this time thinking about New York. You are aware of the new traffic system here and the new developments including the new big-league baseball stadium but you find yourself thinking about the people who live along the route into Manhattan from JFK International, from La Guardia and from Newark, thinking: dog-ass and chicken shit:*

("Sorry, sir, that sign should have been taken down; we have no vacancies. Sorry, sir. I really am so sorry, sir.")

Then in your Peachtree Street hotel room later on you recheck the following entry from the looseleaf notebook you had begun in Lenox Terrace three weeks before: *The way people say things up north may not conjure up the piney woods and moccasin swamps and the sound of the bloodhounds and hooded huntsmen, to be sure; but neither can it be said that all you have to do is make it across the Mason-Dixon to be free at last among nice multicolored neighbors and omni-American friends. Not so long as it goes with policemen who are no less poor white or hysterical for being mostly potato-famine Irish. Not so long as it goes with rat-race–oriented European refugees become Harlem slumlords and merchants. Not so long as such un-Southern talk goes with housing and employment policies that make downhome segregationists seem like bush-league bigots.*

The fugitive slaves found out about forked tongues shortly after the Indians did. Perhaps too many of their up-north raised descendants have until recently preferred or pretended to forget it, but even during the heyday of the Underground Railroad all you had to do was meet a few abolitionists in their Yankee hometowns, in which free Negroes were even more rigidly segregated than in the South, to realize that their fine Christian zeal (not even theirs!) for black liberation did not go hand in hand with any all-consuming commitment to equality of opportunity or to any truly comprehensive conception of pluralism as the ideal for an American social order. And yet no image is more appropriate to the motto E pluribus unum than that of a mainstream fed by an infinite diversity of tributaries.

Perhaps the Yankee sound doesn't evoke bloodhounds and lynching bees because people up here don't say ugly downhome words—not out in public, anyway. They say ghetto instead of niggertown. They say minority group meaning subspecies not only of citizen but of mankind. They say culturally deprived meaning uncivilized—but here they forget that civilization has as much to do with the propagation of crime and perversion as with the refinement of propulsion, glass, aluminum, and ferroalloys.

Nor does it follow that downhome white people display a frankness which is to be preferred to Yankee hypocrisy. Not for one segregated second. It makes some things somewhat less confusing of course but the vicious clarification represented by the old White and Colored entrance signs is hardly better than the confusions of yankeedom. Furthermore, anybody who knows anything at all about downhome white people knows only too well that they are likely to be ever so much more wrongheaded than forthright.

What with all those mulattoes in almost everybody's family closet (and—to be devastatingly fair—perhaps sometimes in the last wills and testaments as well) and what with all those skeletons (not to mention mulatto fetuses) in the woodpile—not to mention the sneaky propaganda concocted about black backwardness, as much to mask as to excuse white savagery—who could ever fall for that old stuff and nonsense about at least knowing where you stand? Who the hell wants to stand in the center of a hysterical mob? What should be realized by now is that those old robes and hoods were really designed to cloak the Ku Kluxers from themselves —and perhaps also to permit the morning-after illusion of shedding the moral consequences of behavior whose perversity insofar as they themselves are concerned is literally unspeakable. So much for frankness in this red-faced neck of the woods.

To which you add:

Robert Penn Warren's point in Legacy of the Civil War *about the South using its defeat as the Great Alibi and the North using its victory as the basis for a Treasury of Virtue is well taken. Yet the North is infinitely less preoccupied with its Treasury than the South is with its Alibi. (Indeed, far from manifesting any enduring pride in its role as glorious liberator, the North is most likely to give the black Southerner the impression that it would just as soon forget the whole thing—what little it remembers to allow itself to remember of the whole thing. That, in any case, is the impression a black Southerner in the North is most likely to get, once he gets beyond all the welfare-oriented do-goodism.)*

That certain New York intellectuals place little emphasis on the Civil War (beyond that required to discuss the fiction of Faulkner) is easy enough to understand; for the most part their native past begins with post–Civil War immigration and that gives them another emphasis. Not that any of them hesitate to draw

77

on the Treasury of Virtue, but in terms that have more to do with Marxian abstractions than with vernacular inheritance.

But what about the old-line Union Army–derived Yankee? How much accrued virtue does he help himself to when none of his civil-rights Blacks are in earshot, and the Southerner says: "Look what y'all done coming down here messing up our good thing and don't care no more for freedmen than we did for slaves?" You can only wonder how many damnyankees would say yes we do and we'll do it all over again.

The next morning you stop in at the Atlanta bureau of the Los Angeles *Times* and meet Jack Nelson, and he puts you in touch with Joe Cumming, the Atlanta Bureau Chief of *Newsweek* magazine, who invites you to meet him at Herren's for lunch. It turns out that Pat Watters and Marshall Frady are out of town, but Reese Cleighorn, formerly of the Atlanta *Journal* and now in residence at the Southern Regional Council, will be free sometime during the late afternoon.

You chat with Jack Nelson about Ralph McGill; about young Julian Bond, whose uncle J. Max you once worked for at Tuskegee. You are pleased to note that Nelson has a friendship with Bond which is intimate enough for him to pick up the phone and call almost as casually as he called Cumming and Cleighorn. But Bond is out of town on a lecture tour; so you and Nelson sit and chat about Mobile and how good the seafood is from there along the Gulf Coast drive to New Orleans; and then about the Charles Evers campaign for mayor of Fayette,

Mississippi, currently in progress. Among the first things you had to notice upon entering his office was an EVERS FOR MAYOR poster on the wall. On your way out Nelson nods toward it and says, "When you get to Greenville tell young Hod [Carter III] I got his stuff working up here."

So you are not at all surprised to find that his article about the return of a black Mississippian from Chicago has none of the old our-darkies-are-coming-back bullshit in it. The Los Angeles *Times* of April 24 ran it under the following heading and sub:

GHETTO DRIVES NEGRO BACK TO MISSISSIPPI;
Growing Political Power, Improved Living
Conditions Preferred to Northern Slums

And it turns out that the Mississippi James Hamberlin (for such is the young man's name) has come back to is the Fayette of Charles Evers.

During lunch Joe Cummings, who is at work on one of *Newsweek's* periodic roundup reports on the progress of the so-called black revolution, keeps shaking his head in compassionate and astonished bewilderment that he still finds such stiff white resistance to changes which he personally regards as being so obviously necessary. Indeed, even as he talks about the amount of legal and political trickery he finds some otherwise very nice people resorting to, he seems to become more and more discouraged—so much so that you begin to wonder if his compassion is not precisely the thing that is obscuring for him the obvious fact that revolutionary changes have taken place and that white resistance to such changes is unquestionably less than ever before in the history of the South. (Before the end of the year there was to be a Jewish mayor, a black deputy mayor, a black chairman of the school board.)

You say: "Man, I don't know. But I think maybe the trouble with most of the reports I've been reading is that they are not really based on the observation of change. I mean what bothers the hell out of me is that they almost always seem to be based on what is essentially only a textbook conception of something called "revolution." I mean most people never seem to realize that the patterns they see in, say, the French Revolution or the Russian Revolution were really superimposed later by historians. People talk about this phase and that phase of this or that historical movement but they forget that such cutoff points were determined much later by historians much the same as acts of a play are worked out by a dramatist. Some of these guys, it seems to me, sit somewhere in an armchair or a classroom reading about events which have been edited, see what I mean? edited, into movements with snappy names, and then they go out and try to write about current events as if they already know what the historical outline is. Well, man, you can't even do that about football—and a football game has an outline that is geared to a stopwatch."

As he chews on that, somewhat surprised but also obviously intrigued, you remember two points you were trying to make in a discussion with a Pulitzer Prize–winning foreign correspondent and a sportswriter one night in

New York: that most war correspondents don't seem to know nearly as much about combat as sportswriters know about the games they report, and that if all you have is antiwar reporters on the one hand and chauvinistic reporters on the other the public is likely to be getting more propaganda than reliable combat information. They were talking about the so-called credibility gap and what you were trying to explain was why so far as you were concerned a news-media report was not necessarily closer to actuality than an official version. (And besides, how could there really be a credibility gap when most people already knew that you never could tell when politicians were telling the truth? They lied to get into office and they lied to stay there.) But what the two writers in New York were really concerned about was not credibility or accuracy in reporting but peace—or rather ending the war in Vietnam. They were very compassionate about that, and so were you. But the trouble was that you couldn't trust their compassion as a source of information. Moreover, wherever it involves Negroes, compassion is forever degenerating into condescension.

To Joe Cumming you say: "To people who really know the game, football is much more than touchdowns, field goals, and conversion points. The real progress report includes the first downs, the yards gained, the passes completed, and a hundred or so other details [including the area of the playing field in which most of the action takes place]. Not to mention all the stuff that adds up to morale and drive. A lot of civil-rights stuff I've been reading makes me think about the kind of sportswriter who sits up there looking right at you piling up more first downs than the other team, completing more passes for more yardage, and playing most of the game in their territory, and then goes off and builds an 'ekes out win' story on the fact that you won by the one touchdown you scored in the last quarter. Of course sometimes it is not that he doesn't know. And sometimes needless to say it is his simpleminded editor's notion of what news is, or rather what a given news story should be. Or take baseball. Imagine a sportswriter who is unable to evaluate the importance of being in a scoring position. Man, he doesn't know the game."

Later when he comes back to the Southern area progress report that he is going to have to file to *Newsweek*, you say at one point: "Let's take this chick waiting this table. Man, she's got to be fresh off of Tobacco Road or some goddam where. So I wouldn't be at all surprised that if you followed her home and interviewed her for *Newsweek* she would express all kinds of negative sentiments about desegregation—a white girl shouldn't have to serve Negroes, and all that crap. She might not, but I wouldn't be surprised if she did. But is what she says when interviewed on desegregation as a specific issue really more significant than the way she is acting right now with me sitting right here? Look man, I'm not about to find more change in white Southern attitudes than a white Southerner like yourself will concede. Not me, man. If you say these cats are getting ready to fire on Fort Sumter again I for one am not going to dispute you. But the point is, I'm not down here to run any statistics but just to see how it feels. I'm operating on my literary radar, this time, my metaphor finder—how about that?—and you know what my goddam radar is telling me about this girl? That she is a country girl, new to the great big city of Atlanta, a young girl from the provinces, the Georgia sticks, come to seek her fortune in the big time, and she was far more concerned about getting our orders right just now than about anything else in the world. My radar indicates that the difference between her embarrassment when I had to help her spell Heineken and when you had to help her pronounce Shrimp Arnoud was nil. She was relieved and thankful. Man, what she is really worried about is some stern-eyed maître d' and some evil-assed cat back in the kitchen! That's not the whole story of course, but it is the part that most often gets left out. Well, I happen to think that attitudes just might be too tricky for the statistical survey in the first place—certainly the survey as we know it. But you know something? I'd be willing to bet that this girl isn't actually running into nearly as many desegregated situations as she had anticipated—and get this—had already prepared herself to accept when she decided to come out of the sticks. And you know something else? I just might be willing to extend that bet to cover the revolutionary emotional reconditioning of a lot of other white Southerners nowadays—in spite of some of the things they still say and still do. Man, I got my fingers crossed but I try to keep my eyes and ears open too. For instance the fact that we are sitting here, instead of somewhere out on Auburn Avenue or West Hunter in the first place. And I must say the fact that it seems to count for so little with you makes it all the more indicative of how fast some things have changed—especially when you look around this room at how people are minding their own business as if they were at the Algonquin or the Café de la Paix or somewhere and then remember how many of their ancestors are turning over in their Confederate graves. Some of whom are not even dead yet, man. Yet they know very well that being here puts me in scoring position, man, football or baseball."

Not that some of the old crossroad-store plus courthouse-square sensibility that you associate with the best white Southern writers isn't reflected in almost everything Joe Cumming says. It is there in the local details he cites reviewing some of the revolutionary/reactionary confrontations he has been observing recently, and you also hear it in the downhome quality of the questions he asks about New York.

On the question of prototypes and self-definition, however, it is not the mention of such Southern journalists as Ralph McGill and Jonathan Daniels that stimulates his most immediate and most personal response. He acknowledges their influence (along with that of Hodding Carter and a few others). But the real shock of recognition comes when you describe yourself as a writer whose nonfiction represents an effort to play literary vamps and intellectual riffs equivalent to the musical ones Duke Ellington feeds his orchestra from his piano:

Oh hey, oh say, you too? Duke Ellington? The Duke? Oh, that man! Isn't he the greatest? Isn't he just absolutely—say, let me tell you something about me and that man. Look, let me tell you something. That was what I wanted to run away from and go up to New

York for. That music. Duke Ellington. Me and another old boy back then. Man, I'm telling you, we were really going. You have all those old records? Me too. Oh man."

So then the two of you sit calling the names of Ellington records and sidemen back and forth to each other as Duke's boys almost always do whenever they encounter each other no matter where: *"Say, how about when. Remember when Cootie and Rex. How about when Tricky Sam Nanton. How about Jimmy Blanton and Ben Webster and Barney Bigard!"* All of which also brings back those marvelous times when it used to be one of the greatest thrills in the world just to be sitting in the Paramount Theatre in Times Square seeing old Ray Nance ("Oh that Ray Nance!") come bouncing down to the solo mike with Johnny and Lawrence and Harry Carney in the background as cool as an Egyptian brown-and-beige pantheon.

But you don't say, Hey, you know something, Duke Ellington was your Uncle Remus. Nor do you say, O.K. so let's hear some Duke on your next *Newsweek* gig. Because when it comes to that, how much Duke do you hear on black magazine gigs, especially from those writers who are most insistently blacker than thou?

Except for a brief visit to the Southern Regional Council to meet and chat with Reese Cleighorn, who used to work for Ralph McGill on the Atlanta *Journal*, you spend the rest of the afternoon sightseeing. Cleighorn suggests, as does Jack Nelson, that the man who knows McGill best is Eugene Patterson, now of the *Washington Post*—but actually you've decided that a McGill story requires more research than you have time to do. *Because along with your memories of his seed-store–feed-store journalistic insightfulness, there is also the image of the newly elected member of the Tuskegee Board of Trustees, sitting alone in sleepless embarrassment at the pedestal of the Booker T. Washington monument at three o'clock that morning with what was left of a bottle of something, complaining that he had less courage than "that black ex-slave up there."*

You look for the old landmarks along Peachtree Street (including Zachary and Muse's the haberdashers which were to the Atlanta of your Tuskegee days what Fannin's was to Montgomery and Metzger's was to Mobile). Then you make your way once more to Rich's bookstore, remembering how it was when you first saw it back during the heyday of *Gone with the Wind*, which was also when Atlanta was trying to be an even older place than it was before the Sherman caper, saying gone with the wind but trying like hell to look as far as possible back beyond the so-called New South of Henry W. Grady all the same.

Then from Rich's you take the bus out to West Hunter to see Atlanta University, Morehouse, Spelman, Clark, and Morris Brown once more, remembering how the fried chicken in Ma Sutton's café used to be worth the trip in spite of the fact that the reason you used to make it was that the downtown Atlanta of those days was so goddam segregated you couldn't even use a clean rest room; remembering also that Atlanta University had also been a part of the so-called New South and that one of its finest graduates was James Weldon Johnson of the class of 1894; and that W. E. B. DuBois during his first period there (1896–1909) had written *Souls of Black Folk* and had also initiated, according to Guy B. Johnson, the first real sociological research in the South.

You also remember how during your days at Mobile County Training School the rotogravuresepia images of DuBois in his satanic goatee, Booker T. Washington (close-cropped, beardless, full-lipped, and without mustache), Frederick Douglass (coin-perfect in his lion's mane), Harriet Tubman in her glorious bandanna, old knob-headed Jack Johnson with his satin-smooth shoulders and tight pants, and all the rest of them used to blend together in a sepia-bronze panorama when the student body used to stand and sing "Lift Every Voice and Sing," which was written by that same golden-brown James Weldon Johnson and his brother J. Rosamund Johnson and which everybody used to call the Negro National Anthem—but which for you was first of all the Brown American national school bell anthem (the comb your hair brush your teeth shine your shoes crease your trousers tie your tie clean your nails rub a dub stand and sit and look straight make folks proud anthem!). So far as you are concerned, not even Martin Luther King—the stamping ground of whose youngmanhood you are treading even now—could inspire his most eager followers to put as much aspiration and determination into "We Shall Overcome" as people always used to get into James Weldon and J. Rosamund Johnson's school bell song.

It is on the campus of Morehouse College not at

SCLC headquarters or even at Ebenezer Baptist Church that you find yourself remembering Martin Luther King most vividly this time.

There is no accounting for miracles, to be sure—and certainly such a good man as Martin Luther King was as miraculous a phenomenon as any that ever came to pass; nevertheless, you like to think that every tangible thing about him was an altogether natural fruition of some aspect of the black Atlanta University system you had learned about during boyhood and youngmanhood in Mobile and at Tuskegee. The charismatic eloquence, for instance, which on occasion enabled him to lead his followers like an adult-oriented and politicized pied piper, was an unmistakable extension of a long-standing local tradition of first-rate pulpit oratory. Indeed, in the Atlanta in which King came to his calling, well-trained activist ministers were as plentiful as, say, big-league saxophone players were in the Kansas City of the young Charlie Parker!

But what strikes you most forcefully as you find your way around Morehouse this time is how specifically King also embodied the very highest ideals of the splendid black, brown, and beige Morehouse Man who whether Alpha, Kappa, Sigma, or Omega was forever dedicated to the proposition that for those precious few Negroes who were privileged to come by it—by whatever means —a college education was a vehicle not simply for one's own personal gain but for the uplift both social and spiritual of all of one's people. (Or at least as many as one's achievement permitted one to reach.) Indeed, even as your achievement raised you above your brothers it also made you not only responsible to but also accessible to an ever-increasing number of them. Not that the Talledega and Fisk traditions, for instance, were any less tightly geared to "service." As a matter of fact, the Hampton and Tuskegee traditions represent the epitome of grass-roots service. But still and all there was a special Morehouse "something," which was made up of many things but which was most impressive—which is not to say obvious—in the way Martin Luther King always kept his cool no matter what the situation, his Morehouse cool and his Morehouse dap. Indeed, in the clutches he reminded you of nothing so much as the Maroon Tiger coolness and "class" that coach Frank Forbes, who himself was always as unruffled as he was well-tailored, always used to require Morehouse athletes to maintain especially under the pressure of imminent defeat in championship competition. King may or may not have served an apprenticeship directly under Forbes but he represented the ultimate extension of that Morehouse something which nobody, not even the magnificent Benjamin Mays himself, imparted more effectively than did Frank Forbes—that something which used to make the Maroon Tigers look as good losing as other teams looked winning! It is not at all unthinkable that some of that played a part in enabling King to achieve nobility, even in the process of being brutalized by degenerate red-neck deputies.

At midnight you sit looking out over Atlanta from Polaris, the revolving cocktail lounge above the Regency Hyatt House, thinking of things you could have added to what you had said to Joe Cumming about measuring revolutionary change. Item: The most fundamental revolutionary changes begin not at the bottom with the so-called masses but at the very top. The place to look for such change is in the centers of power and prestige. Are there any highly qualified but erstwhile excluded people at the conference tables—where policies are made? Are there any in the restaurants, the cocktail lounges, drawing rooms, ballrooms, where the deals and achievements are celebrated? Those, as any competent student of social change should know, are the revolutionary questions. Facts and figures about unskilled and semi-skilled employment wages, housing, and schools are not necessarily indicative of revolutionary change. Social betterment, economic rehabilitation, yes, and by all means. But revolution is something else. Everybody talking about revolution don't mean it. Most media-oriented spokesmen don't even seem to know what a basic change is.

Item: To the statistician a token is something you can write off as being insignificant because it is not big enough. But when you are talking about revolutionary change, tokens and rituals are often more important than huge quantities. The old numbers game is a jolly good hustle for appropriations-oriented social workers, but Southern reactionaries are much more likely to fight about tokens than about numbers as such. Look at the fit pitched by all kinds of noncollege white people when Charlayne Hunter and Hamilton Holmes first entered the University of Georgia. But how big an uproar was and is there about the actual number of Negroes now employed in good-paying jobs at Atlanta Airport? Have any white reactionaries ever taken the trouble to count them? When you desegregate a school or a neighborhood, how many of those white people who flee would stay on upon being assured that incoming Negroes absolutely would not exceed a fixed quota no matter how small? Maybe reactionaries operate on a more profound understanding of or intuition about the functional interrelationship of tokenism and incentive than those ever so compassionate white liberals who are forever insisting that all black people must be equal with each other. It is probably all too obvious to the reactionary that *expanding the horizons of aspiration* has as much to do with liberation as anything else. In any case when the reactionary says, "Who do you think you are, coming in here"; and says, "Let one in and before long there will be a whole slew of them"; and says, "Give one of them an inch and they'll take a mile"; he seems to know very well that expanding the horizons of aspiration is precisely what is at issue. He wants even the smallest black schoolchildren to feel that they will never make it to the top. And yet your compassion-oriented white liberal on the other hand seems entirely unaware of the possibility that when he writes off outstanding Negroes (especially those who move in circles higher than his own!) as tokens he could well be creating an effect on young people's horizons of aspiration that may be even more restrictive than segregation. After all, brutal exclusion often inspires determination, whereas the downgrading of achievement could easily lead to exasperation and cynicism. If all outstanding black men are only token dispensations whose intrinsic merits count for nothing, why should any Negro pupil be anything except a con man?

You wake up on the second morning with still another item: As for those ever so fashionably despairing black polemicists (those who are not hype-artists to begin with) who fall for such cheap white liberal bullshit, they have simply forgotten that U.S. Negroes, not unlike all other people, including Russian and Chinese Communists revolutionaries, want their leaders to enjoy all the privileges and protocol that all other leaders enjoy. Official pomp and circumstance after all is as indispensable to revolutionary power as to established power structures. The so-called masses want their great men to come among their people, yes, a thousand times yes, but they most certainly did not want men like Martin Luther King to be forced to put up with dilapidated segregated accommodations simply because the first-rate hotels wouldn't allow him to enter. What they clearly and justifiably resent is the fact that the white segregationist by his action is saying that even the finest achievement does not qualify a black man to the ordinary things any white man can take for granted. It is not at all surprising that even the black separatists became boiling mad and threatened to burn down Madison Square Garden because several (only several, mind you) Negroes were denied membership in the exclusive $25,000 a year New York Athletic Club. When the NYAC, which was sponsoring the track meet at Madison Square Garden that was the occasion of the protest, pointed to its record of helping worthy athletes, on some level of awareness the black protesters knew very well that helping Negro athletes out of the slums could never really make up for deliberately keeping their heroes from the summit.

Successful Negroes may try to outdo each other in demonstrating to The People that for all their accomplishments and acclaim they are still just folks. But, as perhaps anyone concerned enough to study such matters will no doubt discover, a leader, who is after all uncommon by nature, can only pretend to be a common man. It is sometimes necessary to project himself as a nice guy, a regular fellow and all that, but such is nature of charismatic authority that the so-called common people will not tolerate very much common behavior in their leaders—a public gesture or two, yes, but even so the minute a leader really climbs down off that pedestal the people are likely to replace their awe of his halo—with contempt for his feet of clay. The fact is, when you destroy the people's awe of the leader you also destroy their sense of security in his specialness. Nobody could be more mistaken than those black spokesmen who think that talking down will increase their mass appeal. Acting ignorant as the saying goes may impress certain pseudo-revolutionary white slummers but Negroes are likely to prefer leaders who sound technically proficient. Martin Luther King was not simply a sincere and familiar-sounding minister; he was an *educated*-sounding minister. The ever so down to the nitty-gritty speeches of Malcolm X never brought him the following during his lifetime that his smoothly edited "auto-biography" has built up since his death.

Then as the limousine circles by the Dinkler Plaza on the way to the flight that will take you to Montgomery and the bus to Tuskegee, who do you see coming out of the Alibi Lounge as if on cue? What statistically unique, statistically insignificant, but no less symbolically over-whelming figure betokening the national status of Atlanta as now-South metropolis—in spite of the reactionary forces that produced and support Lester Maddox? Who else except Hank Aaron, looking as barber-shop-sharp as Mobile, Alabama, baseball players have always looked walking that old be-sports-shirted, high-shine morning-before-the-game walk along the main drag, not only as if with Earl Hines' old Grand Terrace Band playing "Cavernism" on a jukebox in the background, but also as if they were really road band musicians in town to play a dance?

You rap on the window, but you don't say *"Hey there, Mobile. What say, home?"* All you do is rap and then wave as from the bleachers thinking: *Hey you some token, cousin.* All you do when he waves back is smile feeling every bit as good inside as you do sitting back watching a pregame warm-up or hearing Duke vamping into, say, "Laying on Mellow" preliminary to bringing on Johnny Hodges.

I see you, Mobile; I see you man, and me, I just hap-pen to be the kind of homeboy that can smell glove leather, red mound clay, and infield grass all the way back to the days of Bo Peyton and Bancy and Tanny, who, as Chick Hamilton must have told you, was without a doubt the fanciest first baseman who ever did it. I see you, Mobile and I don't even have to mention old Satchel Paige, who is not only still around but right here in Alana to boot. I see you, Hank. Three hundred and seventy-five miles from Mobile by way of Boston and Milwaukee plus the time it took Atlanta to make it out of the bushes. What say, home?

FOUR

TUSKEGEE

Triangulation Point Three Five Three Nine

The old place you used to come into coming in from Atlanta by railroad was Chehaw, from which you used to take the Chehaw Special on into the campus. Traveling mostly by air nowadays however you land at either Columbus, Georgia, or Montgomery and come in by bus or private car. The distance is approximately the same from either point. But this time you've chosen the thirty-eight-mile ride from Monkey Town to Skeegum-Geegum because that way yau can stop by to meet and talk with Ray Jenkins.

When you get to the Alabama Journal *however you find that Ray Jenkins is expecting you but because of a story now breaking must stick close to his desk for the next several hours. So you make do with his offer of a brief chat on the spot, and take a raincheck on his invitation to double back later on in the afternoon to continue over drinks somewhere. It sounds great, especially since the only place you've ever done that sort of thing in the Cradle of the Confederacy is out at the officers' club at Air University. But the fact is that even as you find out that he is one of McGill's literal heirs (who sometimes used to stand in for him not only on speaking engagements but also for writing assignments) you are already beginning to visualize the old Greyhound ride along US 80 east with the pecan orchards in the distance as you pull out heading for Mount Meigs and Shorter and the once-more-ness of Macon County.*

On the itinerary the stopover at Tuskegee comes after

Atlanta and before Mobile. But it so happens that any bus you take to get there from Monkey Town will be en route not from but to Atlanta. So now, even as you let the seat back and the bus settles into the old ever so easy to remember heavy-duty-rubber-on-open-country-asphalt road hum that will last all the way from Prairie Farms to the approach to Greens Fork you are all too aware of the fact that you are traveling not south toward but north by east and away from Mobile, even as the two-car basketball motorcade bringing the MCTS Whippets to the Regionals came that spring.

That time which was the first time ever, the route they took out of the Beel and the bay sky and moss plus cypress bayou country in the Ford and the Chevrolet was 43 north through Mount Vernon and Grove Hill and then 5 into 22 to pick up 80 out of Selma. But coming back up again in the late summer of that same year to matriculate, it was route 31 by Greyhound through Bay Minette and Evergreen and Georgiana and then 80 out of Monkey City. Mister Buster Brown college bound don't you let no-money turn you round. Mister Buster Brown from down in Mobile town. Who if not you Mister Buster Brown? Who else if not who ever Mister Buster Brown? And when else if not whenever and how else if not howsoever and ever Mister Buster Brown?

Whoever made it through grade school. Whoever and whoever and howsoever, and from that point on the details were almost always left to you. Not that you were really entirely on your own. You always knew very well that somebody was there and you also knew that it was not only mama plus papa or auntie plus uncle but also and also and also blood relations or no. But even so, such was the process by which they made sure that you were weaned that all anybody was ever really likely to say again was never anything that was any more than something about making something that amounts to something out of yourself.

What they meant when they said it was up to you was don't be the-one to keep your own self down. Find out whatever and whoever it is you want to be and do your level best and you can count on somebody backing you up the best we can even when it's something ain't nobody ever even heard tell of before. Because folks don't necessarily have to be able to use all them big dictionary words to understand life. You just go on ahead and let them see you trying and they'll understand more than you might think. And anytime you don't believe it all you got to do is get up somewhere and mess up and see if they won't know it. "They'll know it all right and you'll be hurting them more than the white folks ever did or ever could."

You were the one getting the book learning so it was you who were supposed to be able to do such articulation as might be required. But the actual truth of the fabulous matter was that very little if any ever was. Nor (the steel-blue actuality they weaned you on being what it was) could you, for your part, ever expect to get away with blaming any of your own personal shortcomings and failures on anybody else, including the white folks —least of all the white folks: Boy, don't come telling me nothing about no old white folks. Boy, ain't nothing *you can tell me about no white folks. Which was to say mean and evil low-down and dirty white folks, whether outright stuck up, downright cruel—or whether two-faced and underhanded. It was as if everybody had always known about all that.*

Indeed, absolutely the last thing in the world you could ever imagine yourself or any other buster brown from Mobile County Training School doing was coming back complaining, "Look what they did to me." (I was going to town but they turned me round.) Because the only one you could possibly blame anything on, even when you did run afoul of white viciousness was yourself. Absolutely the only thing you could possibly come back saying even then was: "I'm the one. That's all right about them, it's me, because I already knew exactly what to expect and I still didn't do what I was supposed to do when the time came, that time. But that was that time, watch me next time."

Mister Buster Brown Mister Buster Brown don't you let nobody turn you round. Ain't always the white folks bust you down. As you were by no means alone in finding out soon enough: Hey you who you little granny-dodging snotty-nosed granny dodger you ain't no goddam more than no goddam body else. Hey you who you going around so stuck up like you so wise and other goddam wise you can't talk to folks since you made it on up there in that little old two-by-four high school?

Not that white people were not almost always likely to try to say something infinitely worse. Nor was white antagonism likely to be mostly only verbal. But nobody ever expected you to grin and bear any more of that than your circumstances absolutely required you to do for the time being. Which was not the case at all when it came to some of the old henhouse stuff some neighborhood folks especially certain street corner woofers and tweeters were forever signifying in one way or another:

Hey you who you how come you got to be the one running your mouth so much and so proper-talking like don't nobody else know nothing just because you passed a test in a book or something. Hey you who you let me tell you one goddam thing mister little-old-know-so-much smart-ass goddam nigger you don't know no goddam more about it than no goddam body else because don't no goddam body give a goddam shit about none of it no goddam how. You can read all them old white folks books you want to and you still ain't going to be nothing but another goddam nigger just like every goddam body else. So don't come getting so goddam bright-ass smart-ass around me goddam it like somebody supposed to think you so much because you over there running up behind some little old Mister goddam-ass Baker and them old hancty-butt goddam Mobile County Training School goddam teachers.

But no matter how terrible some of them could sometimes make it sound didn't "Hey you, who you" somehow or other still mean who else if not you? At least some of the time? Because in spite of the worrisome Sunday school lesson about going unto one's own and having them receive you not, and also in spite of all of the fireside admonitions about the kind of folks who worked against their own folks like crabs pulling one another back into the basket were you not always convinced that a time would come when many if not most would be only too willing to say something else? "That's my goddam boy up there taking care of that goddam business. Hell, I used to kick his little old snotty-nose ass every time he open his mouth anywhere near me. Ask him and ask him if I didn't help make him the man he is today." (WHO THE ONE MAN YOU THE ONE.)

As the Greyhound you've taken this time zooms on out of Sweet Gum curve, you bring the seat back to the upright position and begin checking your watch and calculating the arrival time against such landmarks as you can still recognize (after seven years this time) from there on in. But even as your mounting anticipation sweeps you on ahead to Greens Forks, the old Confederate square and the taxi ride out to the campus and Dorothy Hall, it is as if it is in the pit of your stomach and the seat of your pants that you remember the two pop songs you kept humming and whistling to yourself in Mobile that last summer. One went: "I'm THRILLED/ *I'm so excitingly/*THRILLED . . . /*the* SOMEthing *thing thing thing/ . . ." And the other: "the ashes on the floor/ the way you'd slam the door/I miss them when the day is through/when I sit alone and think of you/and those little things you used to do/ . . ." But it was not really the lyrics as such; it was the way the music, which was only downtown Mobile radio music, downtown Mobile department-store perfume music, movie magazine music, went somehow with your awareness that the time had come to leave home perhaps forever. So all the way to Tuskegee that time it was also the music that went with*

the good-bye that Miss Somebody was all about from
the very outset. Who said, Now I'm going to see. Who
said so far so good, but now you on your own. Miss pre-
"Blue Lou" Somebody, Miss pre-"Big John Special"
Somebody, Miss pre-"Moten Swing" Somebody.

John Gerald Hamilton, who was there from Detroit will
remember what being a freshman was like that first September. Wherever old narrow-eyed, level-talking, pigeon-
toed-walking Gerald Hamilton is now he is not likely to
have forgotten those days, and he probably remembers
that it did not rain very much in spite of two of the
songs that were so popular that year. He will remember
that it was not a very dry and dusty month either, that
along with the late-summer blueness of the central Alabama sky there was a back-to-school breeze that felt as
good to him socializing on the tennis courts, no doubt,
as to you out for football on the practice field beyond
the water tank.

Gerald Hamilton, whose nickname was Jug, not for
Jughead but for jug of wine, as in underneath the bough,
will remember the then rust-red but now silver dome of
Tompkins Dining Hall, the weathered green clock tower,
White Hall lawn, the Band Stand, the old Bugle Stand,
and the whiteness of academic columns as you saw
them through the flat preautumnal greenness of the elms
lining Campus Avenue. Nor will he have forgotten the
brick-red oldness of dormitories like Cassidy, Band Cot-
tage, Thrasher, and the four Emories behind the Trade
School on the Greenwood side of the campus. So he

will also remember the newness of Hollis Burke Frissell Library, the Gym and Armstrong Hall which was already known as the Science Building but which at that time was also where most of the academic classes were held: Math and Physics and Dean W. T. B. Williams' office on One; Biology but mostly English, French, History, Political Science, Social Science on Two; with Three being mostly Chem labs.

Jug Hamilton, whose customary jug in those days was really a Leyden jar and whose wine was most likely to be the traditional chem-lab alcohol–plus–grapefruit-juice cocktail, will remember all of that and also what it was like in the hallways and on the stairways of Armstrong Hall between class bells in that year of *Esquire* Magazine plus road musician and Hollywood-derived swankiness and also how it felt to know at last that going to college was *this*, and going to Harry V. Romm and Raphael Tisdale for Biology; to Ralph N. Davis, Jessie V. Parkhurst, and Charles G. Gomillion for Sociology; to lawyer Albert Turner for History and Political Science; to pipe-smoking chalk-throwing Hollis Price for Economics; to McCormick and his satchel and cigarette holder for Physics; to smiling but relentless Joe Fuller for Math; and to Red Davis whom freshmen were not alone in confusing with a District Attorney for Psychology, and, worse still, Tests and Measurements!

So will Andrew Walker and Cleo Belle Sharpe Walker remember those days, and so will Jack and Dick Montgomery from The Ham and Harold "The Deep" Smith from Memphis and Margaret Young from Selma (a town which once evoked the word "university" as Tus-

kegee evokes the word Institute) and so will Frecks Esk-
ridge of Pittsburgh and Dennison Graine of Kalamazoo;
and so will Mabel Smith and Lulu Hymes from Alana
and Billy Hegwood from San Antonio; Jackson Burnside
from the Bahamas; and Terresetta Glashen there all the
way from Africa. As for Frank D. Godden who delivered the mail, it was as if he was already an upper
classman.

They all will remember W. Henri Payne with his
brownskin Frenchman's mustache whether they took
French or not that year. They will remember Alphonse
Henningburg and his beautiful wife. Nor will anybody
have forgotten that the only way to repeat anything Dr.
Carver said was to imitate him in as high a pitch as possible (adding precisely enunciated dirty words which would
have horrified him: "They ask me: 'Dr. Carver what
makes rubber stretch?' and I say to them quite frankly
I don't cop what the fuck makes that shit act up like
that, I don't dig no rubber-stretching shit. I dig peanuts,
I dig potatoes"). In the case of Cap'n Neely the key
word was *"boy"* with the notorious Neely vibrato; and
then there was Cap'n "Now Now B-Buddy" Love.

Ralph Ellison who was there from Oklahoma City
will also remember those days. But not as an invisible
freshman. He must remember that particular year as
an upperclassman. He will always remember buildings
named for Collis P. Huntington and Russell Sage and
Andrew Carnegie and John D. Rockefeller. He will remember already knowing about such outlying regions as
Rockefeller Hill and Brickyard Hill and Rosenwald
Heights and Eli Crossing, and when as in his novel

Invisible Man he concocts marvelously outrageous anecdotes about a Bitch's Sabbath Juke joint which, not
unmindful of a book by Lewis Mumford, he calls the
Golden Day he may well be riffing on things happening
somewhere over in that vicinity before that September.
But he will remember which autumn you mean because
he was with the band in Crampton Bowl in Monkey
Town for the Thanksgiving Game with Bama State and
that was the year the Bama State Collegians kept taking
off a riff which turned out to be related to "Mister
Christopher Columbus," *with the trumpets reaching and
screeching while a city-slicking Bama State broken-field
runner probably named Red Fields, carrying the ball as if
it were really draped over his arm like a waiter's towel
kept directing his interference as if he had all the time in
the world, as if saying: "Hey, you get this one here and
you get that one there, and I'm taking care of these last
two cotton-picking Booker T's my damn self."*

Ellison, who was not only there as a trumpet player
but was also majoring in music probably still shudders
when something reminds him of the novelty song which
everybody hated but kept singing that winter: *"You
press the middle valve down/And the music goes round
and round/Oh oh oh oh—ho ho/and it comes out here."*
But as a well-established upperclassman with an upperclassman's easy familiarity with members of the faculty
he was also there to be remembered—along with Tom
Campbell, Eddie Hollins, and John Hoskens; along with
Laly Charlton and Thelma Bradley and Sue Whitefield,
not to mention Big Shit Crawford, Catfish Smith, Bull-
dog Smith, Stinky Dog Redmon, not to mention King-
Kong Wingo, Frankenstein Green, and the one and only

Dad Moberly, who had been playing quarterback since the days of the legendary Big Ben Stevenson, the Satchel Paige of football who had obviously been the Four Horsemen plus the Galloping Ghost all in one.

Naturally Addie Stabler and Frank Watkins will remember most of this. And so will Leo Greene and Orlando Powers. Because like you they were also there on scholarship from Mobile County Training School—that being the year it was decided and declared that Tuskegee, not Talledega, not Fisk, not Morehouse or Spelman would get Mister Baker's Talented Tenth. But it is Gerald Hamilton whose memories of the first days in Room A H 202 for English 101 with young Mister Sprague, Morteza Drexel (Hamilton, Howard, Columbia) will no doubt be closest to your own. It is certainly old Jug Hamilton who will best remember the morning young Mister Sprague read from William Saroyan's *Daring Young Man on the Flying Trapeze,* to illustrate how free and natural and expressive of your own personality, your own sense of individuality he wanted everybody's informal themes to be. Because it was old Jug Hamilton himself who was the only freshman who could stroll across to Sage Hall afterwards talking about such un-Mobile County Training School things as free association and stream of consciousness, mentioning such unheard of *avant-garde* writers as James Joyce, Marcel Proust, Virginia Woolf, and Gertrude Stein as casually as if they were boxers, baseball or football players, and movie stars.

It was old Jug Hamilton with whom you shared the copies of *Esquire* Magazine with articles and stories by Ernest Hemingway that young Mister Sprague used to pass along; and it was with him that you play-talked not only he-said-she-said goddam hemingway talk but also finger-raised stage-eloquent Shakespearean iambic pentameter, sword-poised, hip-cocked Cyrano de Bergerac flippancy. Later on it was to be Mort Sprague himself with whom you shared the Auden and the current poems and essays of Eliot and the current Pound, and Kafka and Kierkegaard, and, best of all, Thomas Mann's *Joseph* story. (Nor did he find it in the least strange that your enthusiasm for Thomas Mann's dialectic orchestration went hand in hand with your all-consuming passion for the music of Duke Ellington and Count Basie. He said it proved you were one on whom Chaucer and Shakespeare were not lost and he began a collection of blues-idiom records of his own.)

But before you became an apprentice teacher you were a freshman and it was Gerald Hamilton, whose Sage Hall room looked out from under the eaves and across the fire escape and that part of the campus to the clay-red, pine-dotted hills and besides being the London flat of Sherlock Holmes was as old as any skylight garret in Paris, as fabulous as any workshop in the Florence of Benvenuto Cellini. Old Jug Hamilton's room was where you went when you wanted to be in a place that was as old as the world of Boccaccio or of Chaucer or of Rabelais or Cervantes; or as new and now as the illustrations in Sheldon Cheney's *Primer of Modern Art*, as Einstein and the Fourth Dimension, as the radio and as the candid-camera pages of *Coronet*—*Life* Magazine was yet to be born, *The Literary Digest* was not yet dead —as old as the world of Abelard, François Villon, of

D'Artagnan's Musketeer mentors; but also as new as Louis Untermeyer's updated anthologies of Modern Poetry, as streamlined and functional as the Frank Lloyd Wright plus Alexis de Seversky designs old Jug himself sometimes knocked out for his classes in Architecture.

Meanwhile you were also very much aware of the world of the novels being read for young Mister Sprague's English Four Something Something by Ralph Ellison, Trementia Birth, Letitia Woods and other book-reading upperclassmen, a world which began in the fall with *Moll Flanders* and *Clarissa Harlowe* and *Tom Jones* and included the people of Jane Austen and Thackeray and Dickens during the winter and ended in the spring quarter with the people of Thomas Hardy including Eustacia Vye, Clym Yeobright, Tess of the D'Urbervilles, and Jude the Obscure: somehow from that time on it has always seemed that Thomas Hardy's *Return of the Native* belonged to Trementia Birth and that *Jude the Obscure* belonged to Ralph Ellison. Many books still seem to be the exclusive property of old Jug Hamilton of course, but not even Villon's *Testament* or *Gargantua and Pantagruel* evoke his presence and that time more readily than Rockwell Kent's special edition of Voltaire's *Candide*.

Perhaps Gerald Hamilton, who for some reason seemed more concerned with such matters than other freshmen, will also remember a particular conversation about the relative merits of various prominent upperclassmen, the question being whether they were truly big-league academic caliber or mostly jive artists. Addie

Stabler and Leo Greene will remember and so will Frank Watkins and Orlando Powers that back at MCTS from the ninth grade on the question was one of being of college timber, and of leadership fiber such as would bring credit not only to your alma mater but to all your people.

Gerald Hamilton, who may or may not remember what was said about Joe Lazenberry, for instance, or about, say, Jody Harris (who was pictured in the student handbook as an ideal cadet) but he will hardly have forgotten Sandophra Robinson and Ralph Waldo Edgar Allan Powe, or the day you checked him out as the other Ralph Waldo, the one in Music, the one who sometimes worked at the main circulation desk at the library, wearing expertly tied bow ties, first-quality sports jackets, welt-seamed contrasting slacks, black-and-white shoes, the one you had also seen in Miss Eva K. Hamlin's Art Room modeling a bust of Marie Howard.

"Hey what about that Ellison guy?"

"One Ralph Ellison?"

"You know him? Walks bouncing kinda like that guy that played Shadow in *Winterset*."

"Oh yes one knows one Ralph Waldo–type Ellison. Here from Oklahoma not without some bepuzzlement to one William L. Dawson, composer, conductor, as to one Alvin J. Neely, Registrar and Dean of Men, and to the utter exasperation of one Addie L. Long, housemother. One knows him."

"What about him?"

"Music major, student concert master as it were."

"I see he's been checking out a lot of good books."

"He reads them."

"I mean good ones like us, not just for class."

"He reads. College will not interfere with his education."

"He just finished *Seven Gothic Tales*."

"Then it is evidently readable matter."

"He checks out a lot of poetry too."

"He would."

"Not just Edna St. Vincent Millay. I mean like *Personae*, *The Waste Land*, Robinson Jeffers, and writes some."

"He would do that too."

"I was next to get *Roan Stallion* and there was a slip of paper with some free verse about life and death being two beautiful nothings."

"Ha! No *Hound of Heaven* for this one. The watchful Ellison eyes say otherwise."

"Hey, you think maybe he has read *Ulysses*?"

"He will if he hasn't."

"You think working there they might let him read that copy in that cabinet?"

"Egads, Joyce locked up, with Radclyffe Hall. *Ejoe ejoe am seel!* But back to the matter of one Ellison's commissions to poetry."

"How beautiful are these two nothings."

"Ah, my dear Vatson. Such matters run passing deep as whale shit as 'twere. Yet may the source be as unmistakable as one Cyrano de Bergerac's considerable proboscis. For aren't we all desolate because sick of an old passion?"

"Hey, you mean cherchez les on-sait-bien-quoi?"

"Last night ah yester night betwixt her lips and mine there fell thy shadow, Cynara! C'est toujours Cynara, quoi. And obviously I do not mean one Sue whatshername. Ah Wilderness. *Mais où sont les neiges d'antan?* Dans les pissoirs, I fear. Gone, I fear, with neither a fart nor a fizzle, comme tout les choses, comme ça! But e'en in dissolution is art served. But leave us not wax Baudelarian! For the art of which I speak serves mankind, what?"

Remembering all of that, good old Jug Hamilton, the greatest of all undergraduate pacesetters will probably also find himself remembering a short story by Wilbur Daniel Steele and saying how beautiful with shoes: *"How beautiful are thy feet with shoes, O Prince's daughter!"* Then he may or may not, with or without blushing, also recall a jug-nursing soliloquy which went something like this: Ah but that goddam Ariadne Belle Robinson, one nut-brown wench of Birmingham, the insouciance of whose lips, hips, and shall we say what-the-fuck shall we say? the disturbingly, nay, destructively underslung proportions of whose chassis—beside one knuckle-head John Gerald Horny Ham fat sinking in the inner springs that were Paradise in this neck of the woods, enow."

The best-selling novels that everybody (of the book-reading minority) was reading that year and the next were *Anthony Adverse* and *Gone with the Wind* (and who remembers Lloyd Douglas's *Magnificent Obsession* and *The Green Light?*); so naturally there were those to whom the old Alexander House sitting back in the roadbend just outside the campus beyond Cassidy

Hall and diagonally across from Reid's filling station was Scarlett O'Hara's plantation house, Tara. For most other Tuskegeeans, however, students and local people alike, it was simply another very old ante-bellum place that was not quite far enough gone with the wind, and that they tried to ignore as if it were really a very old some-times sensitive and very embarrassing scar. Mostly, they didn't even mention it except perhaps in giving direc-tions. Mostly, it was almost as if they were pretending that it was completely hidden in the thickets. But it wasn't. It was framed in trees and shrubbery but it was anything but hidden. Indeed, when you were coming back from downtown Tuskegee (known then as now as Tuskegee *town*. There was and still is Tuskegee *Institute*, and there was and still is Tuskegee *town*) the old Alex-ander place with its octagonal tower and red roofs and fluted columns was the most impressive thing you saw. You came directly toward it and until you reached the wisteria and honeysuckle curve and could see the filling station, the cleaners, and the stretch of off-campus shops and the Chicken Shack it looked like a part of the Insti-tute. In fact, white visitors were forever asking: *Is that his house? is that where Booker T. Washington lived? Is that The Oaks?* ("No but it is where Teddy Roosevelt stayed when he came down to visit Booker T. that time.")

Gerald Hamilton not only read and preferred the picaresque (and historic) sweep of *Anthony Adverse* to *Gone with the Wind* before you had, he was the one who pointed out that the expression "gone with the wind' was obviously derived from the third stanza of

Ernest Dowson's (and his very own) "Non Sum Qualis Eram Bonae sub Regno Cynarae" and that it was of course also the inevitable reply to Villon's "Où sont les neiges d'antan?" But to him the old Alexander place was a part of the living past that so deeply concerned, haunted, nay (as he was wont to say) tormented and ensnarled one William Faulkner, then known mainly as the de caydent author of *Sanctuary*—then mostly regarded as a hard-to-read *God's Little Acre* and *Tobacco Road*—but which Jug Hamilton had already read in Detroit and for some reason referred to by its movie title, *The Case of Temple Drake*.

Bookwise, some, maybe most, of the po' whites you saw around the courthouse square in Tuskegee (*town*) were straight out of the smelly, bony-assed, whicker-bill–squinting, nasty-joke chortling world of Erskine Caldwell, the literary enfant terrible of the day, and so some were also out of *Sanctuary* and *As I Lay Dying*. But the old Alexander Place was William Faulkner's very own wisteria-scented and ever more unquiet grove; and when you were reading *Light in August* (the mississippi-dust-dry-beige Harrison Smith and Robert Haas edition with the august light woodcut on the title page) the old Alexander house, architectural details aside, was unquestionably such a place as had rooms such as the one in which Miss Joanna Burden (whose like you for one were to see every time the trustees came to sit—slumped stack-boned and yankee-rich—in chapel) tried to get Joe Christmas to kneel with her: *"Kneel," she said, "I don't ask it. It is not I who asks it."* (She knew nothing of what such kneeling evoked of the stern old McEachern of Joe Christmas's childhood saying: TAKE THE BOOK KNEEL DOWN.) She was completely unaware of what such a request triggered. *"For the last time, I don't ask it. Remember that, kneel with me."*

Not only did the thickets beyond the Alexander place become the Joe Christmas Thickets from then on, it was as if the Alexander House grounds themselves had been planted by Faulkner: *"...for a whole week she forced him to climb into a window to come to her. He would do so and sometimes he would have to seek her about the dark house until he found her, hidden, in closets, in empty rooms, waiting, panting, her eyes in the dark glowing like the eyes of cats. Now and then he appointed trysts beneath certain shrubs about the grounds where he would find her naked, or with her clothing half torn to ribbons on her, in the wild throes of nymphomania, her body gleaming in the slow shifting from one to another of such formally erotic attitudes and gestures as a Beardsley of the time of Petronius might have drawn. She would be wild then, in the close breathing half dark without walls, with her wild hair each strand of which would seem to come alive like octopus tentacles, and her wild hands and her breathing: 'Negro! Negro! Negro!'"*

You yourself not old Jug Hamilton got *Light in August* from the Library first, but when he finished it—having, as was his habit, cut class to hole up Sherlock Holmes style with it and a jug—you had to check it out again and go back through it all over again. (It was also precisely at that time that you decided that you would read Faulkner with as much attention as you had come to give Hemingway. Incidentally, it was in Mort Sprague's October copy of *Esquire* that you and Hamilton—and perhaps upperclassman Ellison too—had read Hemingway's "Monologue to the Maestro.")

"Eh bien," he said, drawing on his Sherlockian meerschaum, "the first thing is not to confuse Joe Christmas with Peola. This guy Faulkner, whom watch, is no soap-opera slick like your Miss Fanny-assed Hurst. Listen, my good man, *Imitation of Life* is a lot of tear-jerking pulp about Peola wishing to be some cock-sucking ofay. But just look at this faulknerian mulatto—" (*Jug Hamilton was the first one to say faulknerian as in faulknerian landscape, faulknerian character and situation*). "This Joe Christmas is not ashamed of his black blood like Peola. He goes around telling people he *thinks* he's got some and he doesn't even *know* it for sure. Miscegenation—some word, what? full of pubic hair—is something very special and very fundamental on the faulknerian landscape, like incest in Greek tragedy. Forget about him saying 'nigger.' That's style, friend. Mark you. Style. Mississippi style but style. And the degeneracy and decaydence, that's all a part of the poetry and drama, friend. Remember "A Rose for Emily," "Dry September," friend. Look, friend. One Willyam ass goddam Faulkner, peckerwood, whom I repeat *rigoureusement*, watch, can write his old Mississippi peckerwood ass off. We're talking about art, friend. ART. Faites donc attention, my good fellow, ART."

When *Absalom, Absalom!* came (abrupted!) that next year, making O'Neill's *Mourning Becomes Electra* look like a little-theater piece, the old Alexander place, which by that time had already become the homestead of the Compsons and the Sartorises (although not yet of the Edmondses and McCaslins) also became the Colfield place and Sutpens Hundred at the same time. Nor could many people have been much better situated than you and Gerald Hamilton and Ralph Ellison on the campus of Tuskegee not only to read and make believe but also to smell and touch the opening to Part II of *Absalom, Absalom!*: "*It was a summer of wisteria. The twilight was full of it and of the smell of father's cigar as they sat on the gallery after supper . . . while in the deep shaggy lawn below the veranda the fireflies blew and shifted and drifted in soft random . . .*"

Mozelle Menefee whose nickname is Moqué (a play on Moketubbe, no doubt) knows that if you had said the old Varner Place in the presence of people who really know Tuskegee they would have assumed that you were referring not to Frenchman's Bend (as in Gee's Bend) but to the grounds on part (but not all) of which stands the Institute. Those who know less local history than local affairs would have taken for granted that you were talking about a local Judge of Probate named William Varner, who was in fact a man on the order of a Sartoris or Compson rather than the father Faulkner created for Jody Varner. Mozelle Menefee, whose memory of wisteria is of deep purple falling over sleepy garden walls in a song being sung by Gwendelyn Persley on a high school assembly program, will remember that particular Varner not only because she grew up in Macon County, Alabama, but also since his is the name of the Judge of Probate on her marriage license.

But of course John Gerald Hamilton and Ralph Waldo Ellison will probably remember the old Alexander place not only because of books but also because of flesh-and-blood grandparents (pre-Hamiltons in Alabama before Detroit, pre-Ellisons in South Carolina before Oklahoma) some of whom were then still very much alive. *Because you yourself could say: This is another one of the kind Grandpa James was talking about when he was talking about the Big House. Such columns are like where he saw the old Marster and them weeping at Surrender. And you could also think: Big Mamma Gipson's smoothing iron, Big Mamma Gipson's crochet rack and quilting frame. And remember: The oldness of the book-pressed dried roses and the mildew smell of Big Mamma Gipson's humpback trunk the week after the burial.*

On the other hand, you were likely to forget that Booker T. Washington, who after all had been dead for only twenty years at that time, was of the same generation as many of these same grandparents (who, come to think of it, only needed to be between seventy-five and eighty-five). Indeed, such was that oldness of Booker T. Washington in chapel on Founders Day that next spring what with the choir singing against the background of the stained-glass windows, what with the words being spoken as if being recited from parchment scrolls, what with his monument outside among the academic cedars, that he seemed to have belonged not to any specific generation at all but to the ages—as did Abraham Lincoln and Frederick Douglass and Thomas Jefferson and Benjamin Franklin.

Even as you sat listening to them reminiscing about

the daily encounters with "him," even as they said "*Mister Washington*," "*Doctor Washington*," as only those who had known him personally could say it, you found it all but impossible to believe that people like Dr. Carver the peanut expert who was then living in Rockefeller Hall and always walked to his laboratory out on the Ag Side (always wearing a green twig boutonniere that somehow only made him look more like an eccentric groundskeeper than the world-renowned chemurgist) was of the same day and time. It seemed absolutely fantastic that Mister Warren Logan, who had only recently retired (and for whom the new gym was named), that this same Von Rundstedt-looking Mister Warren Logan and countless others whom you saw about the city-state of a campus every day were actually older than most of the buildings and streets, even some of the oldest streets in Greenwood. That was every bit as incredible as it was to accept the incontestable fact that Mrs. Portia Pittman (whose Viennese Conservatory background Ralph Ellison remembers from the music school) was the daughter, not the great-great-great-granddaughter, of the shadowy figure of legend you know from the book *Up from Slavery*. As for Booker T. Three, who like Gerald Hamilton took classes in Architecture in Trades Building A, it was mostly as if the III stood for the number of centuries he was removed from a grandfather born in slavery—not generations. *But then such is the miraculous nature of memory and make-believe and hence the very essence of human consciousness that not only do forgetfulness and recollection go hand in hand they are in truth indispensable to each other. Thus,*

*sometimes even in the most immediate press of circum-
stances and consequently for the most urgently pragmatic intents and purposes when you say ante-bellum
you are not only conceiving but also functioning in terms
of something antediluvian—even as perhaps most people
in the United States have long since begun to think "pre-
historic" when they say pre-Columbian—nor is pre-Columbian Europe conceived of by them as being less
aboriginal than the Western Hemisphere before Columbus.*

*Nor is such recollective forgetfulness in any funda-
mental sense unrelated to the reciprocal interaction of
mythology and actuality in the whole question of your
personal identity. For more often than not when you
say: slavery time, folks back in slavery time, Grandma
and Grandpa back in the olden days on the old plantation, you are neither thinking nor feeling in terms of the
literal time involved. You are almost always thinking:
Once upon a time. After all, isn't the oldness of Uncle
Remus, who is of necessity less old than Aunt Hagar
(mother of us all) every bit as ancient as the oldness of
Aesop?*

Such in any case was the nature of the oldness of the
Booker T. Washington whose greatness you celebrated
in chapel those days and whose achievements all U.S.
Negroes were heirs to, and whose mistakes your own
generation would correct. (The one and only Mister
Baker, Benjamin F., had already given the word on that
at MCTS: *"Booker T. Washington sacrificed too much
to expediency. Dr DuBois in his up-north bitterness
spends too much time complaining. The youth of today
must find the golden mean."*) Not even such indefati-

gable chapel dodgers as Blue Collier, Jack Knight, Slam Green, and Daddy Shakehouse Duncan questioned the downright saintliness of Booker T. Washington's dedication to the Cause. There was never any doubt in many people's minds that Unka Booker meant well. Nor was it at all fashionable to accuse your ancestors of betraying you. They did the best they could against all but impossible odds and it was up to you to do better, and the question was could you do as well. Could you pick up and take it on from there?

Nevertheless the here-and-now tuskegeeness of those days (when the blue-serge cadet uniform was known as the Buka T) was also such that back on the upperclassmen's main stem of Sage Hall the noble inscription (chiseled in the stone pedestal of The Monument) which read: HE LIFTED THE VEIL OF IGNORANCE FROM HIS PEOPLE AND POINTED THE WAY TO PROGRESS THROUGH EDUCATION AND INDUSTRY had become: "*Hey lift the veil, man. Hey, man, lift the goddam veil.*" Had become: "*Hey, horse, you know what the man said; Unka Buka say lift that shit, man, goddam!*" On occasion it could also become: "*Hey looka here old pardner, damn man; here I been drinking muddy goddam water and sleeping in a hollow goddam log hitchhiking my mufkin way all the goddam way from chittlin goddam switch to get here and now I ain't going to get to help y'all lift that chickenshit goddam veil because you gone hen-ass-house and ain't going to help me work out this mess for old Red goddam Davis.*" Or from somebody like the one and only Mister Big-Goddam-Double-Jointed-Door-Rolling Door Roller: "*Hey, damn man. Unka Buka say let down your somiching bucket right where you dog-ass goddam at, cousin. Say, that's all right about all that other shit. Say, you take care of this shit, and, man, if I don't have this shit for Jerkins I am going to have to go back home and tote that barge. Ha! ain't them up-north crackers a bitch? Tote that barge! What kind of bullshit talk is that? And old potgutted Paul Robeson up there singing it like it's a goddam spiritual or something. Hey but come on man, let's tote that goddam veil outa my goddam face for Jerkin's goddam English. Hell, man, we can't be letting Unka Buka Tee down."*

That was also an indispensable dimension of tuskegeeness as you knew it in those days, and so was the embers-like glow of the radio dial in the after-curfew darkness of Sage Hall lounge when you sat listening to Duke over the networks from Harlem: a world whose aristocracy also included Cab Calloway, the King of Hi-de-ho; Chick Webb, the stomp master of the Savoy. Then there was Earl Fatha Hines, from the Grand Terrace in Chicago; then Count Basie, who with a contingent of Blue Devils had just succeeded to Bennie Moten's old Kansas City domain. That was the world whose trumpet and vocal proclamations and jests were dictated by Louis Armstrong and which also included such courtiers as Jimmie Lunceford (formerly of Fisk), Don Redman (formerly of McKinney's Cotton Pickers), Lucky Millender, Andy Kirk, and John Kirby. It was also a world which at that very moment was being infiltrated by Benny Goodman with the help of Fletcher Henderson, Edgar Sampson, Lionel Hampton, and a Tuskegee boy named Teddy Wilson.

All that too was a part of what being there was like in those days. And who, having known it will ever forget the tuskegeeness of The Block back then when the best fountain cokes and milkshakes and freezes in the world were made by Alonzo White and the second best by one faculty-jiving student named Happy White? Nowhere could you go and find a more steady flow of out-of-town sharpies, athletes and big-league musicians to jive, wolf, and signify with than in and around the Drag, the Drugstore, and Bill Washington's clothing store, which was known as Harris and Washington in those days. Not even the mainstem of Sage Hall (which after all was only undergraduate stuff as much fun as it never ceased to be) was as much of a charmed circle as The Block—*especially in the Yardley's English Lavender euphoria of that postgame predance twilight time when happiness was simply being there standing not tall as ofay drugstore squares in their rolled-sleeved open-collared white shirts did, but stashed fly in the gladness of your most righteous threads, whether tweed or hard finished, hanging loose like a blue goose with, say, Lunceford's "Dream of You" on the jukebox for background, until White Hall clock chimed the hour when you would pick up the trillies for the stroll to Logan Hall.* Nor will anybody who was truly with it off campus, like say in the outlying region known as the Lion's Mouth, have forgotten that The Block was also the campus headquarters of such fabulous taxicab pundits as were named Big Pete, Rose Harris, Leroy Love, and later, perhaps even after Hamilton's and Ellison's time, good old Bones.

But the very special dimension of tuskegeeness you find yourself acknowledging and celebrating above all else this trip back is that post–Booker T. Washington Liberal Arts emphasis which was the very self and voice of Morteza Drexel Sprague. Not that you were ever remiss on that score, for through all the years since graduation it was always precisely to him that you returned as if homing to the official benchmark and the exact point of all post–MCTS departures: *"Say you know how it always is in the early morning of hemingway's havana with the drunks still asleep against the walls of the buildings before even the ice wagons start rumbling; well, on my way out to the outskirts for my first look at his finca I was thinking about you and old Jug Hamilton, whose favorite hemingway expression was 'goddamn roastbif' which I think he got from one of those early dispatches from the Spanish front, probably from Ken magazine."*

"Say, you remember how it was with Hans Castorp on that long journey—'too long, indeed, for so brief a stay'—up in the Swiss Alps, well as Mozelle and Miqué and I (up there on vacation from Casablanca) were mounting the narrow-gauge train to begin the thrilling part of the journey—not to Davos Platz but to Rigi Kulm—'a steep and steady climb that never seems to come to an end'—I was telling Mozelle about how you and I used to be almost as thankful to good old Alfred A. Knopf and good old Mrs. H. T. Lowe-Porter as to his olympian eminence himself and that we were really there as much because of The Magic Mountain as anything else including third grade geography.

"Man, there we were, me and Ralph and Mozelle and Fanny and Miqué in the Venice of—hell, everybody all the way back beyond Marco Polo—and these Italian clowns were trying to hustle us for three different baggage fees between parking the car and the Grand Canal —us! Man, old Ralph said, "Shit man, let's grab these bags ourselves—we got too many first cousins among them red caps in Penn Station to come all the way over here to get taken by a bunch of two-bit hustlers who wouldn't be able to make it above 110th Street."

And so it also went when you came back from hemingway's spain, and the paris not only of *The Sun Also Rises* and *The Ambassadors* but of everybody (but especially of Josephine Baker and Coleman Hawkins and Sidney Bechet and naturally of Jack Johnson, sitting at a sidewalk café sipping champagne through a straw, probably waiting for Mistinguette: *"The day the news of Korea came I was sitting talking with Sidney Bechet in Rue Vaugirard and he said: 'It might still take the crackers a little while to get the point. But the day is over when one white man can come out on the gallery in his shirt sleeves with a toddy in his hand and tell the natives to cut out all that damn racket.'"*

And so it was when you came back from Saroyan's California and Steinbeck's California and from London and Rome and Athens and Istanbul. And of course New York: *Man, old Ralph has some evermore outrageous stuff going in that thing he's working on. Man, wait till you see it and you'll see why he feels those* Partisan Review *guys are overimpressed with Kafka. We were talking about the title and he said, 'I guess I'll just have to fight old H. G. Wells for it, and if I'm lucky, people will see how much more I'm trying to do with that metaphor—' "*

And this, when Invisible Man *won the National Book Award: "Hey, Ralph has finally met old Faulkner. Listen to what he says in this letter: '. . . Saxe Commins told me to come place my coat in his office and meet "Bill" Faulkner. So I went in and there, amid several bags, was the great man. You've heard the crap about his beat-up clothes? Well, don't believe it. He's neat as a pin. A fine cashmere sports jacket, tattersal vest, shined shoes, and fine slacks, tie correct and shirt collar rolling down! and I mean down, down'. . ."*

"Ralph says white intellectuals keep coming up and telling him that they find it difficult to refute Ras the Exhorter, and he keeps telling them that the answers to old Ras's rhetoric are right there in the book."

And of course there were reports from Hollywood: *"We had just come back to Château Marmont from the Columbia Recording Studios and Gordon Parks was there taking pictures which have yet to come out in* Life, *goddammit; anyway, Duke and Billy Strayhorn were talking about how to revoice the* Nutcracker Suite *for Ray Nance and Johnny Hodges and Lawrence Brown and Harry Carney, well you know; and they were playing back one of the tapes and Duke said: 'Hey Hey Hey no no no what is that?' And Billy said 'That's Tchaikovsky, I left that part like it was. I decided not to mess with Tchaikovsky on that point.' But Duke said 'Oh hell no, he caint do that. That's not the way to get from there to there, not for my guys. Put the sheets for that on the piano we have to fix that tonight.' "*

And this in a note jotted down in the Andover Shop on Holyoke Street off Harvard Square: *Was out at Boston College with Ralph and when old Ralph threw him a soft-voiced steely-eyed signifying question about the relationship between U.S. Negro alienation and certain missing dimensions in American history as traditionally written, old Sam Eliot Morison missed the goddam point comgoddamnpletely and come talking about maybe something happened inside Ralph over the years to make him feel less alienated!*

And among the tidbits that most certainly would have been included this time: *At a party to launch a newspaper (that didn't come off) there was old Norman Mailer disguised this time not as a somewhat white Negro or a Brooklyn Texan but as a Brendan Behan Irishman standing as if with one foot on the bar rail, shoulders squared, pants baggy, stomach forward, elbows gesturing "cheers me lods" with each sip. Somebody said, "Al, you've met Norman of course"; and I said, "Yeah sure," Bogart style; "everybody knows Podhoretz." And old Mailer gave me his best Irish pub wink and did his José Torres bob and weave and said, "He really is a very noyce goy, Podhoretz. A very noyce goy." Or so it sounded to me at any rate. So, I hear, is Mailer, a very nice Brooklyn nice guy. But he tends to confuse being a swinger with being a swaggerer—or so it seems to a downhome uptown boy like me—or maybe it is his admirers who do this. But you know what always seems to get left out of the definitions of Mailer? The fact that his capers never really suggest Ernest Hemingway as he used to seem so eager to have people think but F. Scott Fitzgerald. Take another look at all of his frantic em-*

*phasis on "making it" and see if the image Mailer actu-
ally projects isn't that of the nice-Brooklyn-boy version
of F. Scott Fitzgerald* I mean *once you get him un-
tangled from Thomas Wolfe and Sinclair Lewis, yes,
Sinclair Lewis,* and maybe Upton Sinclair too.

*As for what old Norman thinks of us in print, all I
can say as of now is that instead of taking off our balls
he only wants to relieve us of our brains. He seems to
like our balls even to the extent of painting his own black.*
And a few months later you would have added: *Did you
see that crap old Norman Mailer wrote about us in* Life
Magazine? *He writes a whole big fat article defining
himself in terms of the zodiac (Aquarius this, Aquarius
that and the other) and then turns around and declares
that it is black people who are such lunatics that they
are all shook up because a white man has put his foot
on the moon!) Very nice guy that Mailer or as Jimmy
Baldwin says "A very sweet guy, really." But is he ever
full of adolescent gibberish about us!*

But this time your memories are mostly precisely of
such previous memories. This time the acknowledgments are made not to him but to yourself, and to those
who, like Mike Rabb for example, invariably refer to
him when they talk to you anyway. Because this time
the Morteza Drexel Sprague—who at home was the
husband of Ellen and the father of Carol and then of
Billy and then of Pie, but who from the time when you
first knew him as the young Mister Sprague of English
101 and who for all the obvious differences as well as
the similarities was to become the logical as well as the

mythological extension of the mister benjamin f. baker-
ness of Mobile County Training School—is there no
longer. Is gone—too soon departed—forever. Except in
the memory (and knowing and believing and indeed
even the breathing) of those who in the ironic nature of
such things will miss him most. To you and them—the
absolutely exclusive *you-ness* of his attention as he
knitted his brow smoking and listening saying: *Ah-hunh!
Is that so? Is ... that ... so?* And then saying: *"Incidentally."* Or saying: *"Of course—and incidentally ..."* will
endure as long as the images on that fabulous Grecian
Urn (in *Ideas and Forms*) which so far as his students
during your time are concerned probably belonged as
much to him as to John Keats.

So in mourning this time but with no less celebration
even so. Because the crucial if not definitive good fortune
that is yours for having been a pupil in whom he took
special interest is everlasting. Because such is the comprehensive generosity that all truly great teachers radiate
as much outside as inside the classroom that you will
always rejoice at the mere fact that he was there when
he was. Because such was the literary fallout that the
mere sight of him strolling across the campus (his
shoulders as square as if he had once played trumpet in
a marching band—which he hadn't) almost always with
a clutch of new books and current magazines in the
crook of his left arm or against his lapel—or standing
almost always as if the Hollis Burke Frissell Library
Building were just over his shoulder in the background
(even before he became Librarian) was itself enough to
evoke the whole world of Art and Letters, the world of

the *Saturday Review of Literature* in those days of Henry Seidel Canby followed by Bernard DeVoto; *The Nation* and the *New Republic* (of Malcolm Cowley and Edmund Wilson). In those pre–New York University–Gotham Book Mart days it was as if that were precisely the way André Malraux, for instance, smoked his cigarettes and clutched his corn bread paper magazines of culture and commitment.

And also let it be said for the benefit of all overnight paperback experts on the psychology of brainwashing and black identity that Morteza Drexel Sprague expected you to proceed in terms of the highest standards of formal scholarship among other things not because he wanted you to become a carbon copy of any white man who ever lived, not excepting Shakespeare or even Leonardo da Vinci. But because to him you were the very special vehicle through which contemporary man, and not just contemporary black man either, would inherit the experience and insights of all recorded or decipherable time. Because to him (as to everybody else on that all-black faculty) your political commitment to specific social causes of your own people went without saying. What after all were the immediate political implications of Beowulf, and of all epic heroism? Nor was true commitment ever a matter either of chauvinism or of xenophobia. To him as to the bards, the scops and gleemen in Fall Quarter Literature (201)—as to Mister Baker at Mobile County Training School—commitment involved such epical exploits as penetrating frontiers and thereby expanding your people's horizons of aspirations. To him in those years when no public event, not even an FDR fireside chat, was of more immediate fundamental or comprehensive significance than a Joe Louis fight, there was no question whatsoever that brownskin heroism must of necessity be epical in scope. As for his own personal attitude toward white people, the question in those days was not one of unka-tomming but of sanding: being obsequious in the manner of the Japanese Sandman. *"O.K. O.K. O.K. but now answer me this. Will he sand for the man with his goddam hat in his goddam hand?"* HE WOULD NOT.

Not only will John Gerald Hamilton (*where ever is he now?*) remember the year which began that September without either pop-song rain showers or faulknerian dryness; he will no doubt also remember that morning when young Mister Sprague of English 101 came striding into class, his bearing, in memory at any rate, not unsuggestive of an ellington trumpet player named Arthur Whetsol, wearing a well-cut gray suit with an Ivy League white shirt and a maroon tie and black scotch grain wingtip shoes. Jug Hamilton, whose sleepy eyes seldom missed any details of any sort, will also remember that there was also a package of Camels showing from the left bottom vest pocket. So he may also recall how carefully this young Mister Sprague, who, it so happens, was also the head of the English Department at that time, checked the roll, reading each name from the registration card, looking up saying Mister or Miss (college style!) each time, repeating the last name then the first name and middle initial and then mumbling it to himself, frowning, grandfather style, as he wrote in his temporary roster. Certainly everybody who was there from Mobile County Training School will remember one particular exchange that went something like this:

"Merry, Mister Merry. Mister Merry, Albert L. Mister Albert L. Merry. Is there a Mister . . ."

"Who? Oh me! Oh! Oh yessir. Present. Here!"

"Mister Albert L. Merry?"

"Present. I mean here. MUH-RAY: M-U-R-R-A-Y."

"Yes, Mister Merry. Thank you." Then to himself as he wrote: "Mis-ter M-U-R-R-A-Y, Merry, Al-bert L."

But it is probably good old A-plus prone Addie Stabler, who will probably remember that incident best of all because the very first thing she said in the hall after class was, "Well, how do, Mister Merry? Or is it Mister Marry? Oh, but isn't that Mister Sprague a cutie-pie? How about that little old cute Mister Sprague with his little old degree from *Hamilton* College and stuff?" Then as she zipped on to the stairway someone else passed saying: "Ronald Coleman? Girl, Ronald Coleman never is to see the day."

That is how you now remember the day that was the beginning of all that. But the last time you saw him was not in Tuskegee but in New York. And the time before that was also in New York. That was that time at Ralph's after the publication of *Shadow and Act* which Ralph inscribed to him as "A dedicated Dreamer in a land most strange."

Most strange indeed nowadays, Ralph: *an everso integrated faculty, but a bookstore (where The Drag used to be) featuring the folklore of white supremacy and the filthlore of black pathology!* Oh Hagar-witless alma mater!

FIVE

MOBILE

Mister Buster Brown back in Tell-Me-Tale-Town

Rearrived on expense account this time you take the limousine to the Battle House not so much remembering the stopover in Atlanta as continuing the interior monologue you began months ago back in Lenox Terrace. But thinking, or at least reiterating, this nevertheless: Yes, homecoming is also to a place of very old fears, some mine (perhaps most of which I outgrew growing up) but mostly theirs (which mostly they did not but maybe at last are at least beginning to).

You tell yourself that you are prepared to take things as they come, after all you are on a writing assignment this time. But even before the bellhop straightens up with your bags he anticipates and allays any such misgivings as may be related to those you had pulling into Atlanta.

"Did you have a nice flight in, sir?" he says; which sounds like nothing in the world so much as: "O.K., man, don't be coming down here getting so nervous you going to be forgetting my goddam tip now. That's all right about all that. So you desegregated. Well, good, so act like everybody else then and lay it on me heavy. Hell, you know I'm looking out for you so remember I got a family to be taking care of. And damn man it ain't your money no how."

It is now the Sheraton Battle House as in Statler and Hilton. But in the old days it was *the* Battle House as in *the* Plaza, as in *the* Waldorf-Astoria. It was *the* Battle House as in the one and only best there is, and what you always saw when somebody used to say Battle House Service or used to say Battle House Steaks (precisely as they would also say Palmer House Service or Parker House Rolls, for instance) was a grand crystal Belle Epoque–opulent dining room where millionaires in stiffly starched bibs sat (beside their bunned and corseted Gibson girl–proper wives) holding their solid sterling forks, prongs down, and left-handed, eating plate-sized steaks that were obviously as tender and as succulent as Oysters Rockefeller.

Because when you used to hear the old saying that the Battle House was a place which, like the Pullman cars on the Pan American Limited or the Southern Pacific back in those days, was for no black folks at all and only a very few special white folks, "*A precious few white folks and no niggers at all,*" what you thought about was not complexion but money, prestige, and power; fame, fortune, and finery. Because only a very few white folks were famous millionaires, and perhaps no black folks at all as yet, except maybe Dave Patton, the contractor, whose big house was out on Davis Avenue. But only as yet. And what you always said about all of that was: "*Don't tell them nothing. Don't tell them a thing. Don't tell them doodly squat.*" Because Mobile is also a place of very old horizon-blue dreams plus all the boyhood schemes that are, after all, as much a part of achievement as of disappointment.

As for the part about being a nigger, the most obvious thing about that was that you were not whicker-bill different like them old peckerwoods were, because you didn't look like that and you didn't talk and walk like that and you couldn't stand that old billy-goat saw-fiddle music. So you were not po' white trash and your ears and nose didn't turn red when you were either scared or excited or embarrassed, and no matter how dingy and ashy you got you never looked mangy and when you needed a haircut and didn't comb your hair you were nappy-headed and even pickaninny-headed but when pale-tailed, beak-nosed soda-cracker people got shaggy-headed they looked as sad as birds in molting season. On the other hand, you had to give them this much; mangy or not they would come out on a freezing morning wearing only a thin shirt, baggy ass-lapping pants and low-quarter shoes, but no hat, no coat, no undershirt, and no socks, and just hunch up a little and keep on going like a fish in an icy pond, while you were all wrapped up in coats and sweaters and still shivering. That was something! And some people used to think that maybe having hair that was that much like bird feathers meant that they could also close their pores like a duck against the freezing dampness of the swamp.

It was also obvious that when the peckerwoods said "nigger" they were doing so because they almost always felt mean and evil about being nothing but old po' white trash. So they were forever trying to low-rate you because they wanted you to think they were somebody to look up to; and naturally you low-rated them right back with names like peckernosed peckerwoods, crackers, red-

necks and old hoojers—not hoosiers, but goddam shaggy-headed, razorbacked, narrow-shouldered tobacco-stained thin nose-talking hobo-smelling hoojers ("I'm a black alpaca ain't no flat-assed soda cracker").

When you were looking into the mirror you were the me of I am; and you were always Mamma's little mister misterman, Momom itchem bitchem mitchem buttchem bwown man and Pappa's big boo-boo bad gingerbread soldier boy; and in the neighborhood you were the you of whichever one of your nicknames somebody happened to like; and in school you were the you of your written name. Nothing was more obvious than all of that. Nor was it any less obvious that when somebody called himself or somebody like himself a nigger he was not talking about not being as good as white people or somebody rejected by himself because he is rejected by white people—not at all. He was talking about being different from white people all right, but ordinarily he was mainly talking about being full of the devil and stubborn to boot: as stubborn as a mule, mule-headed, contrary, willfully different, cantankerous, ornery, and even downright wrongheaded. When somebody said, "Don't make me show my nigger"—or "don't bring out the nigger in me," he was bragging about having the devil in his soul. And when somebody said that somebody else "started acting like a nigger" he was not talking about somebody acting like a coward or a clown. The word for that in those days was darky: "acting like a good old darky." When homefolks said that somebody was playing the darky they meant he was putting on an act like a blackface stage clown, either to amuse or to trick white folks. But when they said you were being an out-and-out nigger they were almost always talking about somebody refusing to conform, and their voices always carried more overtones of exasperation than of contempt: "Everybody else was all right and then here he come acting the nigger." Or: "Then all the old nigger in him commenced to come out. You know how mean and evil some of us can get to be sometime."

So what was suggested by the worst sense of the word "nigger" as used by people who applied it to themselves on occasion was an exasperatingly scandalous lack of concern about prevailing opinion, whether in matters of etiquette, of basic questions, of conventional morality, or even of group welfare: "After everybody got together and agreed how to do it, here he come acting the goddam nigger and talking about it don't have to be that way and can't nobody make him if he don't want to. Like some goddam body trying to make him—when all folks trying to do is get together." "That's what I say about niggers. Can't nobody make 'em do right when they get it in their head to do something else. And that's exactly how come the white man can keep us down like this. Because niggers too selfish and evil and suspicious and mule-headed to pull together!"

That was what the worst sense of the word was all about, not what white folks were always trying to say because what they were really talking about was really the best part no matter how bad they tried to make it sound. Because that was the part that went with being like Jack Johnson and John Henry and Railroad Bill and Stagolee all rolled in one. So of course, as nobody had to tell you but once, it was also the part you had to be most careful about: because the mere mention of one bad-assed nigger in a don't-carified mood was enough to turn a whole town full of white folks hysterical. A newspaper statement like "crazed negro [sic] last seen heading..." scared peckerwoods as shitless as an alarm for a wild fire or hurricane. Of course everybody always knew that the newspaper phrase "crazed negro" didn't really mean insane—or even berserk. Sometimes it didn't even mean angry, but rather determined or even simply unsmiling!

Some folks also used to declare that the reason the white folks wanted to lynch you for being a nigger was because when all was said and done they really believed that the actual source of all niggerness was between your legs. They said you were primitive because to them what was between your legs was a long black snake from the jungles of Africa, because when they said rape they said it exactly as if they were screaming snake! snake! snake! even when they were whispering it, saying it exactly as if somebody had been struck by a black snake in the thickets. Bloodhounds were for tracking niggers who knew the thickets like a black snake. When white folks called somebody a black buck nigger they were talking Peeping Tom talk because the word they were thinking about was fuck, because when they said buck-fucking they were talking about doing it like the stud-horse male slaves they used to watch doing it back during the time of the old plantations.

They said black as if you were as black as the ace of spades not only when you were coffee or cookie or honey brown but even when you were high-yaller or as pale-tailed, stringy-haired as a dime-store hillbilly. Because to them it was only as if you were hiding your long black snake-writhing niggerness under your clothes while showing another color in your face, camouflaging yourself like a lizard. Nor did anything seem to confirm their suspicions about the snake rubbery blackness of your hidden niggerness more convincingly than the sight of you dancing. They always seemed to be snake-fascinated by that, even when it was somebody that everybody in your neighborhood knew couldn't really dance a lick.

But even so sometimes it was not so much a matter of terrified fascination as of out and out enjoyment and frank admiration. During the Mardi Gras season, for instance, when the dancing floats were passing Bienville Square and the shuffle-stepping marching bands, say like Papa Holman's, were jazzing it like it was supposed to be jazzed on such a festive occasion, there was always somebody saying something like: "Here they come, here they come; here come them niggers! Goddammit them niggers got that thing. By gyard them damn niggers got it and gone over everybody. By gyard you might as well give it to them, it'll be a cold day in hell before you ever see a durned old niggie and a bass drum going in contrary directions and that's for a fact."

Nevertheless when you heard them saying "boy" to somebody you always said mister to, you knew exactly what kind of old stuff they were trying to pull. They were trying to pretend that they were not afraid, making believe that they were not always a split second away from screaming for help. When they said Uncle or Auntie they *were saying:* You are not a nigger because I am not afraid. *If you were really a nigger I would be scared to death. They were saying:* You are that old now and more careful now so I don't have to be afraid anymore; *because now you are a darky—a good old darky, so now my voice can be respectful, can remember the authority of reprimands that were mammy-black and the insightfulness that was uncle-black, now I can be respectful not only of age—as of death but also of something else: survival against such odds.* "By gyard, Uncle, tell me something, Uncle . . ." *Their fears of your so-called niggerness became less hysterical not when they themselves grew up but when you grew older. Or so it seemed back then. Anyway, all of that was an essential part of how it felt to be a nigger back in those old days. Which was why white folks couldn't say it without sounding hateful and apprehensive! When some old chicken butt peckerwood says nigger this or nigger that naturally he wants to give the impression that he is being arrogant. But if you know anything at all about white folks his uneasiness will be obvious enough, no matter how trigger-bad he is reputed to be.*

This time it is almost as if it is still the time before, which was only five months ago when after an absence of fifteen years you came back in January and found that the neighborhood that was the center of the world as you first knew it had been razed, completely industrialized, and enclosed in a chain-link fence by the Scott Paper Towel Company.

"All of that is Scott now," somebody after somebody after somebody kept shaking his head and saying then; and somebody else after somebody else repeats now.

"The old Gulf Refining Oil yard is still where it was and you probably remember the old creosote plant down off the creek. But just about everything else over in there is Scott. Three Mile Creek to the Chickasabogue, L&N to the AT&N, Scott, all Scott."

Indeed, to you at any rate, it was very much as if the fabulous old sawmill-whistle territory, the boy-blue adventure country of your childhood memories (but which had been known and feared back in the old ante-bellum days as Meaher's Hummock), had been captured in your world-questing absence by a storybook dragon disguised as a wide-sprawling, foul-smelling, smoke-chugging factory, a not really ugly mechanical monster now squatting along old Blackshear Mill Road as if with an alligatorlike tail befouling Chickasabogue Swamp and Creek—a mechanized monster who even in the preliminary process of getting set (to gobble up most of the pine forests of the Gulf Coast states, to turn them into Kleenex (sic!) paper towels and toilet tissues) had as if by a scrape of a bulldozing paw wiped out most of the trees and ridges that were your first horizons. And although you knew better, it was also as if all the neighborhood people who had died since you were there last were victims of dragon claws, and as if those still alive had survived only because they had been able to scramble to safety in the slightly higher regions of Plateau and Chickasaw Terrace.

But even so you were (then as now) back in the old steel-blue jack-rabbit environs once more, and as you made the old rounds you were home again because you could still find enough of the old voices and old reminders to provide the necessary frame of reference; and after all what more did you expect and what else could you expect? Maybe when Thomas Wolfe said you can't go home again he meant because things ain't what they used to be. If so then all you have to do is remember that things never are (and never were) what they once were.

On the previous trip in addition to those you re-encountered once more along the old Bay Bridge Road, along Tin Top Alley and up in Plateau after all those years since the days of Dodge Mill Road and No Man's Land and Gin's Alley, there was Veleena Withers, a teacher over at Mobile County Training School. Her very presence there, even on an almost entirely rebuilt campus, was such that it instantly brought back vividly to mind the days of Mister Baker, Benjamin F. (whom everybody had long since come to revere even while he still lived as if he, and not Isaiah J. Whitley, were The Founder). Not only that, but everything she did and said was evidence of the continuity of the old mister-baker doctrine of MCTS verities. Indeed, she (whom you had known only casually in high school and had last seen not in Plateau but at Tuskegee) was a misterbaker returnee, just as in addition to whatever else you were, you and Addie Stabler and Frank Watkins and Leo Greene and Lehandy Pickett and Orlando Powers were also misterbaker-directed, nay, ordained, beknighted pathfinders and trailblazers specifically charged to seek your fortune—by which he meant the fortune of your people—elsewhere.

(It was Veleena Withers who put you in contact with Noble Beasley, leader of the local civil-rights organization which at that time had the broadest appeal and was making the biggest impact on City Hall. She assumed that you'd want to talk with him not because there was any connection with MCTS—he is from another part of town and is also after your time; she assumed that for you as for her what Beasley's organization was doing was a logical updating and extension of what the local dimension of MCTS was all about back in the old days, and as far as you could make out she was right.)

It was also through Veleena Withers that you reencountered Henry Williams, a MCTS graduate who teaches Welding at the Carver State Trade School. To this day you cannot place him as of those days except very vaguely by that part of his family which you remember as the Godbeaux or the God bolts. What Veleena Withers knew, however, was that he was not only a welder whose knowledge of his trade included a lot of fascinating background information about the wrought-iron ornaments for which the architecture of Old Mobile has long been noted, but he is also a part-time historian whose first-hand field research and personal sense of local continuity were precisely what you were looking for but were afraid that you had come back too late to find. That was how you had come to spend one whole afternoon and part of the next day with an expert on all the old landmarks and homesteads, and early families, including not only those with names like Allen, Ellis, Fields, Keeby, and Lewis whose African grandparents came over on the old *Clotilda*, but also those named Augusta, Coleman, Edwards, Henderson, all great river-boat men during the sawmill era (which lasted all the way into the Great Depression you remember from the sixth grade).

As for what Henry Williams remembers about you there back then, according to him you were one of the all but out of sight upperclassmen about whom there were misterbaker-made legends, one of which was that the reason you had won your scholarship to college was that you were so conscientious that sometimes you had actually worked out your Algebra and Latin assignments by moonlight.

"Man, old Prof Baker would get going about you and I could just see you down there where you used to live, hitting them books with the moon over your left shoulder." At which you had laughed and said: "Boy, I'm telling you, that Mister Baker. Wasn't he something?"

"What the hell was he *talking* about, man?"

"I don't know. We did used to have to turn off the lamp when the L&N roundhouse blew. But I don't know, I might have snuck out to a streetlight or something to finish a translation for Latin. I can tell you this, it was not algebra."

But thinking about it again later and remembering the chapel-time misterbaker legends about your own upperclassmen you find yourself thinking that homecoming is also to the place of the oldest of all pedestals. *Wherever else is that rib-nudging "That's him! That's him! That's him! Here he comes! Here he is! There he goes!" dimension of acclaim, fame, publicity, or notoriety ever likely to be of more profound and of more profoundly personal significance than on the main drag of the hometown of your boyhood and youngmanhood? Not even your name in lights on Broadway (or on the cover of a magazine on a New York newsstand) not even the instant recognition by strangers, not even the satisfaction of seeing your name and image on national network television, is likely to surpass the sense of apotheosis of buttchem bwownhood you experience when the most familiar people in the world, the people you have known all your life, suddenly look at you as if for the first time —as they do when you hit a home run (or, as in your case, save the game by striking out the last batter) as they do when you bring the house down with an inspired rebuttal, or an oration—as if to say, "Yes; man is indeed what he achieves and this is what you are making of yourself—but whoever would have thought that the little boy—the itchem bittchem baby boy we all knew when he was no bigger than a minute—would become if not quite our glory yet, at least a part—if only a modicum— of our hope!"*

Nor did Mister Baker or anyone else permit you or any other itchem mittchem buttchem bwown to forget the proximity of pedestals to pillories and guillotines, the contiguity of apotheosis to ostracism and disgrace. For after all, where on the other hand was failure ever likely to be more bitterly resented and ridiculed, more difficult to bear, than along that same main drag back home? *"Well, goddammit, boy, you messed up and messed us all up. Boy, you might have meant well but you'sure played hell. Shit, boy, you should have been ready. Shouldn't no goddamn body have to tell you that. What the hell you doing up there messing with that stuff and ain't ready? Boy, who the goddamn hell told you to get up there? Boy, they saw your dumb ass coming. Boy, you up there flat-out shucking and them folks mean business. Boy, white folks always mean business with us. Fool, this ain't no goddam plaything unless you already the expert, and know your natural stuff like old Jack Johnson or somebody. And just remember they didn't stop until they brought him down. Folks counting on you and there you up there tearing your black ass in front of everybody and showing everybody's raggedy-butt drawers because you ain't ready. Hell, if you ain't ready yet don't be jumping up there in front of somebody else that is. Just let it alone, and stay out of the way. Boy, you too light behind. Hell, boy, you don't even know how to hold your mouth right to be grabbing hold to this stuff."* (Mista Buster Brown how you going to town with your britches hanging down?)

On the other hand of course there was also Mister Baker's absolute disdain for those who betrayed even the slightest misgivings about going places and doing things that no other homefolks were known to have gone and to have done. "Oh faint of heart. Oh weak of spirit. Oh ye of little faith! Oh jelly fish, oh Mollycoddle! Yes, many are called but few are chosen. Yes, only the pure in heart." (*Young man, you sure better start getting some*

glory and dignity from the common occupations of life
because from the looks of these grades that's what you're
going to be doing.)

The teacher from the old blue-and-white MCTS whip-
pet banner days you pop in on this time is Jonathan T.
Gaines, now principal of Central High School on Davis
Avenue not far from where Dunbar High School used
to be. It is Sunday. He is at home, and he comes slipper-
footing it in arching his brow in a put-on frown as if to
say: "Yes, yes. So here you are as I knew you would be.
Murray, Albert Murray. Well, well. And now, where is
the rest of the class? Where is Addie Stabler? Where is
Frank Watkins and Leo Greene and Lee Handy Pickett?"
Then during the chat he keeps frowning his old tardy-
bell plus binomial theorem frown as if he is still trying to
make up his mind as to whether your high grade-point
average along with your performance as a debater and
an athlete will get you his tough-minded math prof vote
when the faculty next sits in judgment as to who is
college timber. Who has the caliber to carry the MCTS
colors out into The World.

Completely delighted, you think: *Homecoming is to*
a very old MCTS atmosphere, where teachers knew
exactly what playing Santa Claus was all about; and what
they tried to teach was the blue-steel implications of fairy
tales. WHO IS THE QUICK BROWN FOX WHERE IS THE SALTY
DOG.

SOUTH TO A VERY OLD PLACE

Then later in the afternoon driving south along the old Spanish Trail and into the old Creole and pirate bayou country with Henry Williams you say: "About that joke about me and the books in the moonlight, man, one day I came on campus and everybody was congratulating me because the faculty had designated me Best All-Round Student for that year. Then I got to class and looked around for Kermit McAllister and found out that he had been promoted to the graduating class. Man, when I finished Tuskegee, he had finished Talladega in three years and already had his M.A. at Michigan and when I went up to Ann Arbor for a taste of grad school the only thing old Kermit still had to do for his Ph.D. in philosophy was the dissertation. So he was taking a year off to swim, chase the trillies, and read Santayana. The last time I saw him was in the Gotham Book Mart in New York. He was then an associate professor of philosophy at Howard. The last I heard of Addie Stabler she was teaching at Morehouse. I saw old Frank Watkins last in Los Angeles. I forget whether he was about to get his Ph.D. or had just gotten it, but he had some kind of math-and-physics–type job in electronics or aeronautics or something. I was out there with the Air Force at that time."

༶༡༡༦༄༅༑༄༅༡༄༅༑

You make the old rounds answering the old questions and accounting for your whereabouts and involvements over the years not only as you did the last time and the time before that but also as everybody has always done it for as long as you can remember; and this time that part (which along with the old street-corner hangouts and barbershops also includes gate stops, yard visits, sitting porch visits and dinner-table reunions) goes something like this: "Hey, look who's back down here from up the country again. Ain't nobody seen him in umpteen chicken-pecking years until last when was it, last January? February? Last Feb, no, January. And now here he is again. Like somebody was saying I hope ain't nobody up there after him or something. Oh, oh, excuse me. Hey-o there, New York? Unka Hugh and Miss Mattie Murray's Albert! What say man? Used to be little old Blister from down in the Point. Hey, you looking all right, boy. Don't be paying no mind. Hell, you a Mobile boy, Murray. Ain't nobody nowhere, I don't care where they come from, got no stuff for no Mobile boy unless he get up there and forget where he come from. Hell, just remember when you come from here you supposed go any goddam where and make it."

"All I say is this," somebody else says winking, "just don't be making none of them northern boots nervous by getting too close to their white folks, especially with all the fancy book learning you got. Man, that's the one thing they subject to run you out from up there about— taking their white folks away from them. Man, you might as well be messing with somebody's wife or something! Man, them northern Negroes love their white folks, and don't you forget it."

"Especially them that always so ready to get up somewhere talking about the black man this the black man that," somebody else continues grumbling as much to himself as to you and the others. "Man they'll run over you getting to some old white folks. Man, I used to know some there won't even give you the time of day until they happen to find out that you know some important-looking white folks."

"New York, hunh?," an old poolroom sage comes up slaps you on the shoulder and says, "Hey, say, how about old Cleon Jones and Tommy Agee and them up there with the Mets. From Mobile County Training School. Putting old County on the big-league baseball map. You see that fine brick house old Cleon built over there not far from school? But hell, Mobile is a baseball town, you know. Look at old Willie McCovey out there in Frisco with the Giants, out there with Willie Mays from right up there in The Ham. Not even to mention old Hank Aaron."

"Say, I got a glimpse of him when I stopped off in Lana the other day," you say, nodding. He goes on.

"Old Hank is something else, boy, and from Mobile all the way. Right out there in Whistler! Remember old Emmett Williams and them Hamilton boys? Mobile always has been a mean baseball town. Even before old Satchel Paige, and that was like goddam! I can still remember him with them old Satchel foots up there on the Chickasaw ball diamond forty some odd years ago throwing the stew out of a ball called the goddam fade away. . . ."

"Hey but let me tell you something else about some of them old New York City Negroes," a former MCTS upper classman says. "Man, I remember when I was running out of there to Chicago on the New York Central back in the Depression. That was back when somebody was always hinting and whispering and winking and carrying on about the C.P., talking about the Communist Party. Man, party some stuff. Man the party them New York City Negroes I used to know were talking about was a sure enough party having a ball getting in some frantic white pants. And don't think them fay boys not doing the same thing vice versa. Man but here's the joke about that part. Them fay boys strictly out to get some ashes hauled and them supposed to be so educated boot chicks up there so busy putting on airs because they so sure they screwing their way into some high-class culture, they been had before they catch on that them fay boys think they all a bunch of cotton-patch pickaninny sluts! And, man, talking about snowing them, man all some lil old raggity-butt WPA fay boy used to have to do was take one of them to a cheap concert or a free museum or something and tell them he respect their *mind. Man, was I drug!*

"Man, but what I'm talking about is most of them New York Negroes didn't bit more care nothing about no Communism than they did Einstein and didn't know no more about it. I know what I'm talking about because I was hitting on a few of them fay frails my damn self and they'd leave you these pamphlets and I used to read some of them, and I tried to talk to some of them Harlem cats. Man them cats look at you like you carrying a violin case or something. But the minute they round a bunch of ofays don't nobody know nothing about it but them."

"Hey, how you doing, homes?" somebody else on another corner begins. "Up there in New York, hunh? But hell, all I got to do is look at you looking all classificational and I can see you taking care of business. You really looking good there boy. I kinda lost track of you there recently. We all remember you from over there at the school, you know. So we used to hear about you up at Skegee, and on the faculty and then you went to the Air Corps in the war. See what I mean? And then back to Skegee and then back in the service and traveling everywhere. Then I lost track and then that other time they said you were in here from New York so when I heard it this time I said, 'Hell, I remember that boy, I'm going over here and meddle him a little.' He know me. So how you doing, homes? Goddam, man. Sure good to see you."

Sometimes it also begins in a stylized falsetto exactly like this: "Hey, damn, man, they told me you were here and looking all clean, like for days. So now look here! I got to talk to you, man. So come on and get in this old struggle buggy and let's circle over by my place and say hello so the folks can see you and have a little taste and shoot the goddam shit awhile. I ain't going to hold you long and then I'll drive you anywhere else you got to go. Man, damn, I got to talk to you because I want to know what you think about some of this stuff I been thinking about. I know you might think I'm crazy like some of them say. That's all right. Just tell me what you think. Some of these folks around here, goddam. Some of them. And I say some of them, look like they think they got to latch onto everything come along because it's new.

And it ain't even new. That's the killing part. It's old as all these old country-ass sideburns and bell-bottom sailor-boy pants and pinch-back used to be called jazz-back suits that come in back there right after pegtops and them box-backs. They think they getting with something so cool and all they being is ass-backwards. So all you got to do is just tell me what you think, like somebody been somewhere and seen something and got some sense! Because some of this stuff. Man, I'm telling you."

You go of course. You meet the folks and settle down in the parlor. Then he continues, beginning with an eye-cutting, elbow-nudging button-holing intimacy: "So now the first thing is this, and like I say you might think I'm crazy too. But just think about this for a minute":

Then in an italicized conspiratorial whisper: "*White folks don't go around trying to make fun of us like they used to.* You noticed that shit? Think about it. Now the minute you think about it you got to remember when we were coming along you couldn't do nothing without them trying to make out like somebody so goddam ignorant that everything was always funny as hell. Remember all that old Hambone stuff they used to have in the papers, and all that old Stepinfetchit and Willie Best and Mantan Moreland stuff in the goddam movies and that old Amos and Andy stuff on the goddam radio, all that old Kingfish and Lightnin' and Madame Queen stuff. That's the kind of old bullshit they used to try to pull on us, remember, and we used to see it and, hell, we knew exactly what they were trying to do. You know that. So we went on about our goddam business. So now my first point is this. *How come they ain't making fun*

157

of nobody no more? Wasn't nothing funny about what we were doing and them sonbitches used to write up every goddam thing like everybody talking some kind of old handkerchief-headed dialect. My point is ain't nobody never cut the fool like some of these clowns we got these days and you don't see no crackers laughing. That's what I'm talking about. You used to get somewhere and you were not about to make no mistake because that's what they were waiting for you to do and they would look at you buddy as much as to say, Nigger, you done tore your barbarian ass. So you didn't get up nowhere until you could cut the mustard. Hell, you're not supposed to rip your drawers. Now that's what I call some goddam black-ass pride! That's just what I'm talking about. That's exactly what I'm talking about, cutting the goddam mustard. We got some out-and-out fools will get up anywhere nowdays carrying on with all them old passwords and secret grips like old-time lodge members back when most folks couldn't read and write. Talking about right on and tearing right on through their BVD's to their natural booty holes! And then talking about pride! And them crackers ain't even cracking a goddam smile. So now, you know what I think?"

Whispering again: "*I think them goddam white folks know exactly what they doing and they know if they start laughing and correcting them, most of these clowns subject either to shut up or wise up and straighten up!*"

Normal voice: "So see what I mean? You see the big difference, don't you? Look, don't nobody want nobody laughing at us, you know me, cuz. I'm ready to kill some son of a bitch come trying to make fun of me. So in a way it's good, but in another way you better think about it. I say they ain't laughing because they want us to follow the ones that's so loud and wrong. You get my point? Because if they start laughing at them that get up there talking all that old diaperical psychological economical bullshit they know good and well the others won't follow them. So they don't. Man, white folks the very ones encouraging them to be loud and wrong, man. And that's the problem. Because, see, these fools think you can get up there shucking and won't nobody know it—and the white man working day and night figuring out ways to stay ahead of us. Now am I shitting or gritting? Am I facking or just yakking?"

You say: "I know what you mean. I know exactly what you mean." You say: "Man, sometimes I get that uneasy feeling that rapping is getting to be the name of the whole goddam game for more and more of us." You say: "Old-fashioned street-corner woofing and simple-ass signifying and that's all, and then in Harlem they go around later on bragging about what they said and how it shook up the whiteys and broke up the meeting."

Then in an uptown-mocking voice that is part West Indian, part New York Jewish intellectual, part Louis Armstrong, you say: "I told them, man. You hear me telling them? You heard me rapping. I said like this is the black communertee and black people radicalized and tired of all this old shit from the sick, racist establishment! You heard me. I said 'Forget it, Charley.' I told it like it nitty-gritty fucking is, man. I said, all this old honky shit ain't a thing but some old jive-time colonialism versus upward mobility and black identity. I gave

159

them whiteys a piece of my cotton-picking mind. I said 'Black is beautiful, baby, and you better believe it, chuck.' "

But the main purpose for making the rounds this time is to listen. And later on in another part of town somebody else says: "One thing the old folks used to worry about all the time. They were always talking about education, and saying when you got that in your head you had something couldn't nobody take away from you. But they also used to worry about bringing up a generation of educated proper-talking fools. Remember how folks used to look at you when they said that, and start talking about mother-wit and don't be putting on no airs? Well, we got the finest bunch of young'uns you going to find anywhere in this country these days, but when you look up there on TV you got to admit we got ourselves a whole lot of loudmouthed educated fools to watch out for among them too. Ain't no use in lying about it."

And somebody else says: "Now I'm just going to tell you. Now this is me and this is what I think and I been thinking about this for a long time. All right, so we the ones that got them to open up them schools to our children. That was us, and nobody else and we ain't never said nothing about letting nobody in there that wasn't qualified. Never. You know that. Never. So what do they do? I'm talking about the goddam white folks now. They come up and figure out how they can let a lot of loudmouth hustlers in there that don't belong in there. Because they know good and well these the ones ain't going to study and ain't going to let nobody else study. So that's what we got now. We send them up there to learn what them white boys learning about running the goddam world and they up there out marching and wearing all that old three-ring-circus stuff and talking about they got to study about Africa. Now what I say is if that's all they want to know they ain't got no business up there. That's what I say. Because the white man only too glad if they rather learn about Africa instead of how to run the world. I say them Africans already know about Africa, and what good is it doing them? Every time I see one he over here trying to get himself straight; and most of them hate to go back, and I don't blame them."

To which still someone else adds: "This is what I say. I say we know this white man. I say don't nobody nowhere in the world know this white man better than us, and this is the goddam white man that runs the goddam world. That's a fact, gentlemen, and ain't no disputing it. Don't nobody nowhere do nothing if this white man here don't really like it. You remember what Kennedy did to old Khrushchev that time about Cuba? Old Kennedy said, 'I'm going to tell it to you straight, pardner.' He said, 'Listen horse, cause I ain't going to tell you but once, so listen good or it's going to be your natural vodka pooting ass.' He said, 'Now I want all them goddam missiles and shit out of there by Wednesday (or Thursday—or whenever the hell it was—) and he said, 'I want them back on them goddam boats heading in such and such a direction, and then goddammit when you get to such and such a latitude of longitude I want you to stop and peel back them tarpaulins so my bad-assed supersonic picture-taking jets can fly over and inspect that shit and then I want you to get your Russian ass out of my hemisphere and stay out.' That's this white man, and don't nobody mess with him, and what I'm saying is we the ones that know him inside out and been knowing him inside out. What I'm trying to say is we right here in the middle of all this stuff that everybody else in the world is trying to get next to and what these college boys got to do is get something to go with what we know about this white man. What I'm saying is he smart enough to go all the way up to the moon and we know he still ain't nothing but a square like he always was, so what these college boys got to do is get ready to take all this stuff we know and push it up to the nth degree and use it on this white man right here."

"Now you talking," somebody else continues, "now you saying something. Talking about Africa, this white man right here is the one you going to have to come up against, don't care where you go. And we already know him. Supposed to know him. Better know him. And all y'all know I been saying this for years. Every time some-body come up with some of all that old West Indian banana-boat jive about the 'block mon' I tell them, and I been saying it all these years and ain't about to bite my tongue. I tell them, ain't nobody doing nothing no-where in Africa and nowheres else that this white man right here don't want them to do. I tell them. Every time a goddam African put a dime in a telephone, a nickle of it come right over here to this same white man. That goes for them Germans and Frenchmen and English-men, all of them over there and them Japs too. So you know it goes for them goddam barefooted Africans. So when they come up to me with some of that old monkey-boat jive I tell them: All y'all want to go back to Africa, you welcome to go. Fare thee goddam well, horse, I say. But I tell you what I'm going to do. Because I know what's going to happen. I say: I'm going to get my college boys trained to go to New York City and Washington, D.C., and get next to something. Because what's going to happen is them Africans going to take one look at them goddam jive-time Zulu haircuts and them forty-dollar hand-made shoes and they going to lock your American ass up in one of them same old slave-trading jails they put our ancestors in, and they going to have you writing letters back over here to this same old dog-ass white man in the United States of America asking for money. Hey, wait. Hey, listen to this. Ain't going to let them get no further than the goddam waterfront. They go lock them up with a goddam Sears, Roebuck catalogue. I'm talking about right on the dock, man, and have them making out order blanks to Congress for Cocolas and transistors, and comic books, cowboy boots and white side walls and helicopters and all that stuff. And you know what the goddam hell I'm going to be doing? I'm going to have *my* college boys sitting up there in Washington and Wall Street with a mean-assed rubber-assed goddam stamp saying Hell, no! Saying, forget it, cousin. Hey, because by that time with what we know we supposed to have this white man over here all faked out and off somewhere freaking out and I mean for days! And I'll bet you this much any day, we'll have this white man over here faked out long before any boots from Harlem fake any of them Africans out over yonder.

You go over there trying to pull some old chicken-shit Harlem hype on them Africans and they subject to bundle your butt up and sell you to them A-rabs. Man, them Africans ain't going to never pay no boot like me and you no mind as long as they can do their little two-bit business directly with this same old white man that we already know fifty times better than any African, and I ain't leaving out no Harvard Africans."

You think about all the tourist-style trinkets so many naive U.S. black nationalists seem to think is the great art of the mother country, completely ignoring all of the art history and criticism that goes into museum acquisitions. You also think about how *shared experience* has been a far greater unifying force for so-called Black Americans than *race* as such has ever been to the peoples of Africa. It is not the racial factor of blackness as such which is crucial among Africans any more than whiteness as such kept the peace among the peoples of Europe. But all you do is shake your head laughing along with everybody else.

And what then follows you remember later as having been not unlike the leapfrogging chase chorus exchanges among musicians running down a theme on some of Lester Young's early, post-Basie, combo recordings: the soloists trading eight-, six-, and four-bar statements (nor did they lack any of old Lester's querulous coolness, nor any of his blues-based determination to blow it as he felt it and heard it regardless of what was currently hip):

"Hey, man, me, man (*One trumpetlike statement begins*), you know how come I don't be paying no mind to none of that old talk? Because they talking but I'm looking and listening too. They talking all that old Afro this and Afro that and black this and black the other and I'm right here looking at them cutting up exactly like a bunch of goddam rebel-yelling crackers cussing out the Supreme Court. If you want to know the truth, sometime when some of these TV cats get going about liberation I get the feeling the only freedom they want is the right to cuss everybody out."

"Hey!" (*this could be another trumpet, say with a parenthetical mute, or it could be an alto, or a getaway tenor*), "hey, but you know something else some of this old stuff put me in the mind of? A big old-fashioned church mess. You know what I'm talking about. Look, everybody going to church to try to save his soul and get to heaven. That's what getting religion is for and that's what the church is about. At least that's what it's supposed to be about. And that's exactly how come some old church folks the very ones make me so tired. Everybody in there because they trying save themself from torment and look like all they trying to do is trying to tell somebody else what to do and when you don't let them run your business they ready to gang up on you in some kind of old conference and blackball you out and if it's left up to them right on into eternal fire and brimstone. You see my point? I'm talking about church members now. I'm talking about the very ones suppose to be living by the word. They the very ones always subject to come acting like they already so close to God they got the almighty power to do you some dirt. Man that's what I can't stand about all this ole brother and sister putting on they got all out in the streets these days. The very first thing I think about when somebody come up to me talking about bro is, here come another one of them old deceitful hypocrites."

"Well, now," (*this is plunger style trombone jive*), "talking about rebel-yelling crackers, I'm just going to come on out and tell you, me. Hell, if I'm going to be some old damn peckerwood, I'm going to make sure to be one that's got enough money to play it cool. Damn, that's the least I can do. Of course, you know me. I always did think like a millionaire, myself. I'm always out to make me some more money, myself."

"You and me both" (*you remember this as a baritone statement, barbershop Amen corner baritone*), "and I'm going to tell you something else. I'm going to tell you what they doing. I'm going to tell you exactly what they doing. Because they doing exactly what they always doing when they start talking all that old Mother Africa bullshit. Any time you hear them talking all that old tiger-rag jive about the black man and Mother Africa you just watch and see what the first thing they do going to be. The very first thing they going to do is start turning on one another. Man, you gonna have a much harder time getting two dozen of them cats on a boat going to Africa than they had dragging our forefathers over here. But what I'm talking about is some of these little rascals already getting up calling somebody nigger in front of white folks, and supposed to be getting college educated! Up there shucking and signifying while them white boys knocking themselves out qualifying!"

"And don't think the white man don't know what's happening, horse" (*signifying monkey trumpet, with a mute plus derby!*). "Because you see the white man is the one that knew exactly how we got our black asses brought over here in the first goddam place. Up there talking about black history. I'll tell you some goddam black-ass history. This is the kind of black history the white man studies. As soon as them Africans get mad they subject to take and sell one another to the white man. They been doing it. They been doing it, and they still do it. I keep telling these little rascals it ain't going to do no good calling yourself no African. You got be from the right tribe or whatever it is. Hell mess around an come up with the wrong tribe and that's your behind, Jim. Sheet, the man just about know all he got to do is wait, because just like you say, some of these little fools already up there denying their own folks."

"That's what I say." (*So on it goes and maybe this is a big tenor. But then all the words were there long before the instrumentation.*) "That's exactly what I say. And I ain't talking about criticizing. You got a right to criticize anybody you think doing wrong, I don't care who they is. That's for my own benefit. That's for everybody's benefit. I'm talking about denying your own folks just because you mad with them about something. That's what I'm talking about. I talking about them little fools up there denying their own mamas and papas. I bet you don't hear no young Jews up there calling their old folks kikes, and yids, and Hebes and dirty Christ-killers in front of other folks. Don't care how mad they get with one another. Them Jews got organizations to take care of that kind of old loudmouthed bullshit. Don't take my word for it. Ask New York. Tell them, New York."

167

"Hey wait a minute. Now this is what I say about that. I say ain't nobody going to never get nowhere disrespecting your mama and papa. I might not go to church as much as some folks but I believe in the Good Book and the Good Book say honor thy father and thy mother."

"Didn't it though. Oh but didn't it though. That thy days shall be long upon the land which the Lord thy god giveth thee. I can still hear old Elder Ravezee preaching that sermon when I was a boy."

"And don't forget old Reverend Joyful Keeby. Talking about Africa, I bet you one thing. I bet you ain't nobody going to catch nobody like Plute Keeby talking about going back to his kinfolks somewhere over in no Africa, and old Plute and them can trace their African blood right back to that old hull of the *Crowtillie* out there in the mouth of the Chickasabogue."

"Man, I want to thank you for putting that in there. I just want to thank you. I only want to thank you. I just want to thank you one time. But hey look here now —you know I thought one of y'all was going say when he said that about the boat going to Africa. I thought somebody was going to say something about them northern city boys always talking about Africa and can't even spend a weekend in the goddam country. Man, the minute them cats get off the edge of the concrete, they start crying for Harlem. Now if I'm lying come get me, cousin."

"Hey, yeah, but wait a minute I'm still talking about these little fools getting up there trying to put the bad-mouth on their own dear folks for the goddam white folks. That's putting your own goddam self in the god-dam dozens without knowing it. You see what I'm say-ing? And talking about putting the cart before the horse! Man, damn! Who ever heard of the chillun putting bad-mouth on the old folks?"

"Thank you. I just want to thank you again. Because that's the Bible again. Talking about the sons of Ham. That's laughing at thy own daddy's drunkenness and nakedness. And that's exactly how come the Lord ban-ished his dumb-ass ass to the goddam black-ass wilder-ness. And told him: Here you come all puffed up on something you read in some old book and laughing at thy father who gavest thee the very eyes thou seest with and the very tongue thou mockest him with, and don't know the first frigging thing about what that old man been through to get you where you at today!"

"Showing out for white folks. That's all I say it is, mocking your *own* folks to impress some little old white —and I'm talking about some little old *bullshit* whiteys that ain't got no more than nobody else. That's what I'm talking about. Somebody ain't into nothing with no profit at all. Somebody can't even do nothing for them-selves. So you know they can't do nothing for you. But get you in more trouble than you already got."

"But now you see that's why it didn't surprise me a bit when they broke up with all them that used to be down here every summer two or three years ago. You know what I mean? If you want to help I say thank you. I say thank you very much. But don't come acting like you know more about my goddam business than I do and don't come expecting me to prove nothing to you like you better than me. Hell, ain't nobody better than me. Not if I'm the one telling it."

"That's exactly why I said what I said. I said come on, man. I said goddam. I said what the hell I'm doing wasting my goddam time proving some kind of old bull-shit point to some little bullshit ofays down here on a summer vacation and sicking me on the goddam police to get some knots on my head and they can go home to papa and that fat-ass checkbook any time they want to. So here I am with a bunch of hickeys on my knuckle-ass head and they back up there bragging about how they helped me. Dig that. I said, man, what is this shit? I said man, fuck that shit."

"Hell, anytime they get a toothache Papa can send that private plane down here with his own private doctor on it."

"Yeah, you right. I see what you mean. But I wasn't talking about all of that. I was talking about them jive-time missionaries that come down here just wanting somebody to think they more than they is."

"You goddam right. Me I just don't want no bunch of eager-beaver ofays coming down here telling me what to do just because they might know how to type up a letter. That's one goddam thing I learned in the Army. Don't take no Ph.D. to know how to fill out them papers. You see what I'm talking about. If you supposed to be so goddam white I'm expecting you to put me next to some-thing—otherwise forget it. Anybody can fill out them old papers."

"Well goddammit me, I'm talking about *all* of them.

I'm talking about I don't have to be proving nothing to nobody. Unless I'm trying to get him to hire me. And you *know* I'm forced to be bullshitting him then, bullshitting them a *while*. I'm talking about our children the ones supposed to be leading this thing. Because if you don't watch out them little old ofays will have you all bogged up in some of that old Beatle shit, man."

"Hey but you know where the Beatles got that shit from. You know that's our shit they fucking up like that."

"Yeah, but damn, man that ain't what I'm talking about now. Hell, you know what I'm talking about. I'm talking about some little old chalk chick come talking about the Beatles and all that old rockabilly stuff. You suppose to put her hip. Tell her that's some old nowhere shit for days. Don't be come repeating some old psychological jive like it's deep just because you laying some little old fay broads that's oooing and aaaing over it because they read about it in a goddam magazine."

You say: "I think I know what you mean about the white kids, and yet they may be the first generation of white people who are really beginning to be uncomfortable about their heritage of racism. You have to give them that. But the goddam problem is that they are still no less condescending than their parents. I mean who the hell are they to be 'helping' somebody? How the hell would they know who to help anyway? Goddam it if they really mean business they've got to stop acting as if only the most confused, uninformed, and loudmouthed among us are for real. And everybody else is either stupid or is trying to pass for white."

"Ain't that a bitch," somebody says. "That is a *bitch*, gentlemen. That's a bitch and ahalf. I'm talking about how white folks can always come up with another kind of excuse to be against something look like it might profit us something."

But mostly you listen as if from the piano. So mostly what you say is very much like playing ellington and basie style comp chords. (Remembering also the old one which goes: if you don't play them just pat your foot while I play them.) But every so often it is also as if they have swung the microphone over to you for a four-, six-, or eight-bar bridge or solo insertion. This time somebody says: "Well, what you got to say about it there, Mister New York. Where the hell they getting all this old bullshit up there talking like their own people the ones trying to hold them back. Ain't no goddam body doing nothing but trying to make it *possible* for them. That's what the old folks did for us and mine always told me the way to thank them is do the same for the next generation and any child of mine get up there saying I ain't done my part is just a bigmouth lie and I bet he won't tell me to my face. Just let one of them dispute that to my face."

And somebody else cuts in as with a plunger-style trombone to say: "Hey, especially when you get your head bad. Man, goddam, I'd hate to see one of them little clowns forget he ain't talking to one of them simple-ass ofay reporters and jump you with your head bad. Great googly woogly!"

You say: "They don't really mean it." You say: "I don't think they realize what they're saying. The big thing with them nowadays is to sound revolutionary. Which is fine. But most of those I've talked to tend to confuse revolution with community rehabilitation programs. A lot of them keep talking about what they are going to do for the people of the black community, and I keep telling them that too many of them are only sounding like a bunch of hancty social-welfare case workers, and ofay case workers at that. Man, you go around to the Ivy League campuses and listen to some of our kids talking all that old blue-eagle jive and they sound like they've never been anywhere near their own people. You know what I mean? Like, well, when you come right down to it they sound almost exactly like a bunch of rich or passing-for-rich white kids ever so hot to trot into the Peace Corps. You know what I mean? To help the poor natives somewhere. What bothers me and this really bothers the hell out of me is that they are responding to what they read instead of what they know, and yet when you check them out on what they read you find they haven't really read very much."

"And got the gall to come thinking they so hip," somebody says.

"Hip?" somebody else says, "Did you say hip? Come on, man. How the hell they going to be hip? They ain't been around long enough to be hip. Ain't been far enough. They ain't been into enough. Come on man. How they going to be hip up there showing how much they don't know every chance they get because they ain't hip enough to cool it because somebody *else* might know. Damn, man, the first thing about being hip is being hip to how hip the other fellow is. Man when you hip the first thing you know is you ain't never supposed to be playing nobody cheap just because they come acting like they don't know what's happening. Man, the last thing you can say for these clowns is they hip; and the way some of them going they ain't going to live long enough to be cool enough to be hip and subject to get a lot of other folks messed up in the process, and just over some old loudmouth bullshit."

Elsewhere you yourself also say. "You know what I want them to be like? Our prizefighters. Our baseball players. Like our basketball players. You know what I mean? Then you'll see something. Then you'll see them riffing on history because they know history. Riffing on politics because they know politics. One of the main things that too many spokesmen seem to forget these days is the fact you really have to know a hell of a lot about the system in order to know whether you're operating within it or outside it. What bothers me now is that they are so quick to start formulating policies before double-checking the definition of the problem. The difference between riffing and shucking is knowing the goddam fundamentals. Man, when I see one of us up at Harvard or Yale I want to be able to feel like you used to feel seeing Sugar Ray in Madison Square Garden or Big Oscar there, or Willie Mays coming to bat in an All-Star game. You know what I mean? I like to think that old Thurgood Marshall came pretty close. At one time when he opened his briefcase in the Supreme Court it was almost like Lawrence Brown and Harry Carney unpacking their horns backstage at Carnegie Hall."

Then for outchorus: "Man, if you don't know what to do with that kind of black heritage you're not likely to know what to do with any other kind either. Some of our kids now seem to think that heritage is something in a textbook, something that has to be at least a thousand years old and nine thousand miles across the sea. Something you can brag about. Some fabulous kingdoms of ancient African tyrants for liberation-committed black U.S. revolutionaries to be snobbish about! And yet few would regard themselves as antiquarians. Ordinarily, they're the last people in the world to be messing around with something that is the least bit out of date."

You also find time to sit and listen to what some of the very oldest among the old heads from the old days want to tell you about the condition of contemporary man in general and about the state of the nation's political well-being in particular. Because missing that part, which is always like coming back to the oldness of the old chimney corner even in summer, would be perhaps even worse than missing another chance to sit down to a full-course spread of old-time home cooking once more.

You never miss that part of it if you can help it, and this time (which is chinaberry-blue Maytime) one very special back porch after-supper rocking-chair session in the fig-tree–fresh, damp-clay–scented twilight which is supposed to be about the first three months of the Nixon administration turns into the following unka so-and-so monologue: "Lyndon Johnson. Lyndon Johnson. Old Lyndon Johnson. They can call him everything but a child of God as long as you please and I still say old Lyndon Johnson, faults and all. They talking about what they talking about and I'm talking about what I'm talking about. I'm talking about the same thing I always been talking about. I'm talking about us, and I say old Lyndon Johnson is the one that brought more government benefits to help us out than all the rest of them up there put together all the way back through old Abe Lincoln. I'm talking about Lyndon Johnson from down here out there in Texas. And they tell me old Lady Bird Johnson is from right here in Alabama. The Lord spared me to live to see the day folks been talking about ever since my own daddy, God rest his soul, was a boy and he used to say it back when I was a boy and old Teddy Roosevelt sent for old Bookety Washington to come up and have breakfast with him in the White House that time. Everybody got to carrying on so about that, and my daddy kept telling them over and over. He said, them northern white folks grinning in your face in public don't mean nothing but up to a certain point and beyond that point it don't mean a blessed thing. He said they generally more mannerable toward you than these old pecks down here. You got to give them that but that don't mean they don't expect you to lick up to them if you want something from them. And then they still ain't going no further than up to that point, and they ain't going that far if they got to buck up against any of these old white folks down here to do it. And I said the same thing when you yourself wasn't

nothing but a little blister of a boy. When they all used
to get to making such miration over old Franklin D. I
said that's all right about Muscle Shoals and Three Point
Two and God bless Miss Eleanor for being as nice as she
is and all that, but I said both of them come from up
there and I don't care how good they talk you just watch
and see if they don't always manage to find some old
excuse not to buck the Southern white man. Oh I ain't
going to say they don't *never* buck him. I'm talking
about bucking him in the favor of *us*. So anyhow this
is what I got from my daddy, and his daddy ran away
and fought for freedom with the Union Army, and I
said you can say what you want to, and I might not be
here to see it, but it's going to take one of these old
Confederate bushwhackers from somewhere right down
through in here to go up against these old Southern
white folks when they get mad. My daddy used to say
it over and over again. So when old Lyndon Johnson
come along and got in there on a humble—and, boy that's
the onliest way he ever coulda made it into there—I was
watching with my fingers crossed because he was the
first one from down in here since old Woodrow Wilson
and all that old dirt he did to us—and them white folks
up north not lifting a finger against him either, talking
about old Woodrow Wilson. So anyhow, like I say I was
watching him and the first thing I could tell was that
them white folks up the way was the very ones that was
satisfied that old Lyndon Johnson was going to be like
old Woodrow Wilson all over again. But now here's
what give the whole thing away to me. These white folks
down here. Boy don't you never forget they always been

the key to everything so far as we concerned. So what give it away to me was them. Because they the very first ones to realize that old Lyndon Johnson meant business when he said the time is here to do something. And didn't nobody have to tell them what that meant because they already knew he was one of them and if they made him mad he subject to do some of that old rowdy cracker cussing right back at them, and some of that old cowboy stuff to boot. When they commence to telling me about how mean he is that's when I tell them, I say that's exactly what we need, some mean old crackers on our side, for a change. That's when I commenced to feel maybe the Lord had spared me to see the day, and then the next thing you know them northern folks up there talking about you can't put no dependence in him no more. The very same ones that used to trust him when they thought he was another one of these old crooked Confederates. Now wait, I'm going to tell you what put us in that creditability gap you been reading about. Talking about the government lying to them about something. Boy the consarn government been lying to *us* every since emancipation. Now here they come talking about somebody lying! You remember that old Kennedy boy was the one started talking about getting a black man up there in the Cabinet with him. All right now you got to give him his due for that, but look at the way he up and went about trying to do it. He looked over all them Cabinet jobs he already had open and come talking about if he could just get a new one to fill; and then he come right on out and told them who he was going to put in there—like Congress going to be ever so mighty glad to give him some kind of brand new extra job so he can give it to one of us! Confound the luck, that didn't make no sense at all to me. Then old Lyndon Johnson come along and said he needed that same extra job. But you notice he didn't say a thing about who he had a mind to put in there? And naturally they don't just come right on out and ask him because they know good and well he know how come they didn't give it to Kennedy. So all they did was just kinda hint around to let him know—since he was a cracker anyway. And all old Lyndon Johnson did was wink a cracker wink at them and change the subject. And then as soon as they give it to him he turned right around and put the same one in there they turned Kennedy down on, the same one! That's how Weaver got to be the first one in there. That's why I say you got to give old Lyndon Johnson credit. Because all he had to do was let them know he was going to hold the line on the black man and he could've stayed up there as long as he wanted to. All he had to do every time one of us started acting up was just put on his old head-whipping sheriff's hat and make out like he getting up a posse or something, and theyd've *kept* him up there till he got tired of it. That's why I got to give him credit don't care who don't. Because I know what he coulda done and I remember what he did for a fact. He got up there in front of everybody and said we shall overcome. Boy that's enough to scare white folks worse than the Indians, boy. But you know what that put me in mind of? I'm going to tell you exactly who that put me in the mind of. Old Big Jim Folsom on his way to Montgomery. That first time, I'm talking about. Old Big Jim Folsom talking about y'all come. You remember what Old Big Jim Folsom said when they come up to him about what was he going to do about us? Old Big Jim Folsom told them. Old Big Jim ain't never been nothing but a Alabama redneck and never will be, but he told them. He said what y'all always running around scared of them for? He said, they been right here amongst us all this time. He said, I ain't scared of them. That's exactly what he said. He said, Hell they just trying to get along the best they can. He said now a fact is a fact and they got something coming to them like other folks. He said live and let live. That's what he was talking about when he said y'all come. And that's when these Alabama peckerwoods took his credit away from him and started calling him Kissing Jim. That's what all that's about, boy.

"That's what old Lyndon Johnson kinda put me in the mind of when he got in there—old Big Jim before he went bad. Somebody come in there and told him, 'Mister President, I swear I can't find no experts that know what to do about them niggers being so lowdown and don't-carified.' Now this northern city joker wasn't talking about nothing but getting up some more of all that pick and shovel stuff from back in the days of old Franklin D. Boy, the last thing that joker want to see is a whole lot of our educated ones like you up there getting somewhere like everybody else. But that's exactly where old Lyndon Johnson stepped in. He know good and well all this northern joker trying to tell him is niggers just will be niggers as far as northern white folks is concerned. But I can just imagine him saying, 'Hell, how come ain't nobody tried this: Send me old Thurgill Marshall. He already whipped everybody that'll go before a judge with him. So cain't nobody say he ain't ready. I'm going to make him my chief lawyer for a while and then I'm going to ease him on up on the Supreme Court bench and let him help make some decisions. Then I'm going to put one up there with them millionaires on the Federal Reserve Bank to help me keep an eye on the money. I want him to be a real black one so they can't say I just put old Thurgill up there because he's damn near white! And another one over in the World Bank to look out for that. Make that one brown.' Think about that, boy. Two niggers watching white folks count money!

"Boy, Old Lyndon Johnson say, 'Before I get through I'm going to let some of my niggers get a taste of some of all this high class stuff.' That's what I'm talking about the Lord sparing me to be here. And I can imagine another one of them coming in there and saying, Now, I'm just going to have to come right on out and tell you Mister President, the big money folks up North getting nervous. And that's when I can imagine old Lyndon Johnson cutting into a big red apple with his silver-plated Wild West pocketknife and offering him a slice like a chew of Brown's Mules chewing tobacco and saying. 'You go back and tell 'em I'm from down south so I'm kinda used to having them around me. Tell 'em I feel kinda lost if ain't none of them around. Tell 'em they'll get used to them in here just like they already used to them cooking and running them elevators. But tell them they can depend on one thing. I ain't going to

put nary a one in nowhere unless he ready, and if he
don't cut the mustard I'll kick his black tail out of there
so fast he'll be shame to even remember he was in there.
Tell them they can depend on that.' Boy that's another
thing about so many of them white folks up north. You
tell 'em folks hungry and all they can think about is
spoon-feeding somebody.

"The Lord spared me to be here to see that day. Talking about when old Lyndon laid it on them. But son, I
never thought I was ever born to witness the day that
followed, and I'm talking about followed before anybody could even get set to get something out of what we
were just about to get up close to. Now that's another
thing you got to give old Lyndon Johnson credit for, because you know good and well he must have meant
business because he got too much sense about politics
not to know there was bound to be some white back-
wash. But the thing of it all was the next thing. Because
I been here all this many years and I declare before God
I just couldn't believe it, and I know my daddy poor soul
turned over in his grave. The next thing you know, some
of our own folks up there jumping on Lyndon Johnson
with both feet just like we in with the white folks
against him, and all the time these old white folks down
here just sitting back laughing and talking about they
been knowing niggers didn't have sense enough to grab
our chance if somebody gave it to them.

"So now do you see what I'm talking about, young
fess? Because I said all of that there to say this here. Because you know good and well I ain't talking about
what happened to old Lyndon Johnson. Old Lyndon

Johnson can take care of Lyndon Johnson, ain't no doubt about that. I'm talking about what's happening to us. I'm talking about some of us up there so busy showing out for them northern white folks we done completely forgot what we supposed to be doing for one another. I'm talking about y'all up there doing what you doing and here come all them old nice grinning northern white folks and that's all right with me if they want to help out but the next thing you know they got y'all up there doing everything they talking about. Boy, you old enough to remember when they come grinning down here back during the time of all that old Scotchbug mess. Well, y'all up there putting more dependence in them right now than anybody down here was near bout to be putting in them back then when most people still suppose to been still ignorant. So I said all fhat because I want you to remember this. Just remember you got all your good book learning because that's what the old folks wanted you to get and they want you to see just how high you can go. But they don't want you to get up there and forget your common sense just because two or three of them people feel like grinning at you and treating you nice. You don't have to just flat out and insult nobody. Folks expect you to know better than that. They come grinning to you. You grin right back at them if you want to, that ain't nothing but manners and decency. But just keep remembering they grinning about what they grinning about and you grinning about what you grinning about. You see what I'm talking about old Lyndon Johnson? Boy, I ain't talking about no friendship. I'm talking about knowing what to do when you got your chance to do business with a politician that ain't going to back up off these old Southern white folks because he one of them. I'm talking about what old Lyndon Johnson had to back up off of was the big-money northern white folks. And now we got old Nixon. So now the northern white man come trying to make out like he so worried because old Nixon ain't doing enough for us. But now you just wait and see how many of them going to buck up against old Nixon. Just wait and see. Don't be surprised if old Nixon don't have do more on his own than any of them old nice grinning Northern white folks ever going to be willing to try to force him to do. I'm talking about for us—ain't talking about that old war over yonder. I say it still going to take somebody like old Lyndon Johnson from down around somewhere in here and the Lord might not spare me to see that come around another 'gain but I just hope and pray that enough of y'all will know better next time."

You hope so too. And you want to believe most of what he says about white southerners like Lyndon Johnson as much as he apparently wants to believe it. (*"Some mean ass crackers on our side for a change, for whatever goddam reason"*) But even so if you were naming the "other folks" who would be the ones most likely to stick their necks farthest out for you out of a sense of moral obligation—and keep it out there even against the opposition of their "own people"—most of them would probably be Jewish. Not only that but, Air Force buddies aside, you actually found it somewhat less embarrassing to have to ask urgently needed personal favors of Jewish friends than of white southerners.

Not to mention Yankee do-gooders. On the other hand you'd much rather have old Willie Morris, for instance, go on functioning in terms of his Yazoo City courthouse square sense of actuality than have him become another compassionate pop-cause-oriented, underdog-loving, petty cash-generous, tax write-off neo-Great White Father.

You hope for that too. But you do not ask even that of him, either—or of any other white Southerner, including old Lyndon Johnson himself. Because it is not something for which you ask (and make yourself beholden!). It is not something to be requested anyway; because, as old Lyndon seems to have come to realize as few others have, it is something already required of him— as much by his own personal predicament as by the state of things in the nation and the world at large.

Some altogether pleasant reencounters also go exactly like this: "Is this who I think it is? This ain't who I think it is. This can't be who I think it is. Boy, is this you? Boy, this ain't you! Come here and let me look at you, boy. Look at him. Boy, you something! You think you a man now don't you! Well I guess you turned out all right! They tell me you been some of everywhere and doing all right for yourself, and you sure look like it. Been all over there in Paris, France, and Rome, Italy, they tell me. And Casablanca and all out in Hollywood. And living up in New York these days. Well go on then, Mister

World Traveler, I hear you. Go on with all that old fancy stuff they probably taught you in Paris and Casablanca. That's all right with me. Just don't be up there thinking you so much, and forgetting where you got your start. Because some of these same little gals you left down here in poor little old countrified Mobile, Alabama, don't be backing up off none of them, and that goes for any of them little old clippity clopping bouncy-butt cuties up there in Harlem too. So go on, I know you down here on business and ain't got time for no foolishness but just don't be forgetting. These old Mobile girls never is to be standing still neither."

Other such reencounters begin in the same manner, and perhaps as often as not the topic is also essentially the same. For instance: "You got yourself a wife and family? How come you didn't bring your wife so folks can meet her? Now don't be coming down here leaving her up there because you done gone and married some little old white gal—unless she rich and stand for something. And I'm talking about with money's mammy. But shoot, I know you better than to come doing something like that. Your folks ain't worked themselves down to get you all that good education to be taking care of no old pore-tail white gal with. Boy, if you can't marry no white gal that's rich enough to take care of you, forget it. I know you better than that. So is your wife from somewhere down in here? Is she nice? I'm satisfied she pretty. So bring her on down here with you next time, ain't nobody going to bite her."

"I know she educated and I know good and well she pretty," echoes somebody else who was once almost as certain of her own pulchritudinous plurabilities. "Because you probably forgotten me but I remember you all right. You and Leo Greene. Neither one of y'all ain't never had much for no ordinary-looking broad to do—not in the light of day, I'm talking about. Because wait. You know something? Now, I'm going to tell you something. I said I was going to tell you this one of these days, and I am: So you know something? Sometimes you and old Leo Greene used to go around like y'all were trying to be so cute or something. Especially sometimes when somebody didn't stay on in school. But I think I can just about make you remember a few things, Mister Albert Lee Murray. I just about think I just about can."

You assure this one that you remember very well indeed. *But never as you will always have to remember somebody else who will always be Miss Somebody. Who looked like Kay Francis would have looked if Kay Francis had been sugar-plump brown like that with a shape like that and could have walked that kind of sugar-plump walk wearing bunny-rabbit bedroom mules to the store like that; somebody who said: "Not if you ain't going to stay out of the streets and promise me not to lose sight on the whole world because you finding out what that's made for, not if you ain't going right on keeping that head in them books where it belong"; who said "Lord boy you better not be letting no little old conniving gal come whining your name in your ear so she can come back whining something else soon enough unless you want to end up around here in one of these old sawmills or on the chain gang or something"; who said,*

"boy God knows you ain't nothing, but a child to me,"
and said: "Ain't nothing but a little old boy I don't want
to see getting too mannish for his own good."

But the mention of Leo Greene also makes you remember the time when Mister Baker started talking
about The Ifs of Initiative Ingenuity and Integrity during the morning assembly period and went on and on
about the vision and stick-to-itiveness of great men as
contrasted with the self-indulgence of mediocre men
(with everybody squirming and wondering) until after
one o'clock; and then saying: "Who is going to lead our
people into the great tomorrow if promising young men
like Leo Greene and Albert Murray don't hold their
talent and integrity firmly in clutch instead of riding
bicycles all the way over to Cedar Grove to seduce girls
on Monday of all nights. Ambition must be made of
sterner stuff sterner stuff sterner stuff."

There is also time this trip to revisit some of the old
downtown landmarks: and since you are already staying
at the Battle House you begin in Bienville Square, *where*
the sound of the oldest of all wrought-iron municipal
fountains immediately evokes Hernando de Soto and
Ponce de León once more as it always did during your
grade-school days. (When what used to evoke Bienville
and Iberville was the powdered wigs and slippers and
pastel stockings of Felix Rex and his masked courtiers
during Mardi Gras season.)

188

From the Square you cross Dauphin Street to Kress (better known as Kresses) which is not only the original of all five-and-dime stores but as such was also your actual prototype of all storybook bazaars, including the getting-place of Christmas toys. (There was a time when it was all too obvious that the route to North Pole and the toy workshop of Santa Claus was through the attic of Kresses.) This time the soda-fountain counter is no longer for whites only, and the palest of all paleface girls are now free to smile their whing-ding service with a red-lipped perfume-counter–faced whing-ding smile at you too (in public). And say: "Coke and one burger comin' *right* up." And say: "Be anything else? Well thank you *kindly*, now." And say: "Come agayhan, now, you hear?" democratizing and howard-johnsoning you at one and the same time.

You also stand on the corner of Dauphin and Royal once more remembering how when you used to stand there in that time many years ago waiting for the trolley car, with Checker cabs and chauffeur-driven Cadillacs and Packards and Pierce Arrows passing, when what with seeing so many different kinds of people and hearing that many different languages all around you because there were ships flying flags of all nations docked at the foot of Government Street, only a few blocks away; and what with the newsboys chanting the headlines against the background of the empire state tallness of the Van Antwerp Building you knew very well that where you stood was the crossroads of the world.

From Dauphin and Royal you also circle through Metzgers remembering adolescence as the age of Hart,

Schaffner and Marx and Society Brand and Kuppenheimers plus Nunn-Busch for some and Florsheim for others. The mere sight of L. Hammels and Gayfers reminds you of the time when the theme-song of every high-school Cinderella was "Sophisticated Lady." You stroll remembering and taking pictures along the waterfront and along Government Street. Then finally you have also checked by the Saenger Theatre and found not only that the old side street "Colored" entrance is now closed but also that the movie of the week is something called *Riot* starring Jim Brown (even as during your high school days it used to be Johnny Mack Brown the old Rose Bowl star).

Then before you move from the vintage Mobile oldness of the Battle House to spend your last night in the newness of the refurbished Admiral Semmes, from which the next morning you are to begin the return trip to New York—by way of New Orleans, Greenville, and Memphis—there is one other sidewalk reencounter: "Hey, well, if it ain't old Murray. Am I right? Albertmurray. I got you Murray. I know I got you. Albert Murray. Used to live in that shotgun house down there on the way to Dodge's old shingle mill. Had a chinaberry tree in the front yard and a red oak in the back and then some thickets. Boy when did you get back to this neck of the woods? Boy you sure ain't changed a bit have you? Say who you been pitching for since you left town, Murray?"

"Pitching?" you say, stretching your eyes like Duke does when somebody mistakes him for Cab Calloway and asks for Minnie the Moocher instead of The Mooche. "Man, the last time I pitched a baseball game was back when they were still playing up on old Plateau diamond. Where they used to hit left-field home runs across the Southern Railway crossing toward the Telegraph Road and Chickasaw Terrace. Man, you were probably there. And when they hit hard enough to right center it could go on past that tree and into Aurelia and Louise Bolden's yard."

"Boy, you used to could pitch your tail off. Hell, if you'd come along a little later you could have made it to the majors. Except damn when it comes to batting you couldn't hit a sack of balls from somebody that didn't have near bout as much stuff on it as you. Man, if you coulda hit like you used to could chunk and field. But that's right I do remember you also used to play all them schoolboy games too, like old Sonny Keeby, and stayed in school and went off to college, to Skegee. Yeah I remember now. That's right. Hey, who you coaching for, Murray? You got any of your boys up there in the big money yet?"

SIX

NEW ORLEANS, GREENVILLE, MEMPHIS

Two Moviegoers,
Some Shucking on the Delta,
Some Stuff You Got to Watch and
Some Business to Take Care of

The first thing about New Orleans in the old days used to be that it was the next and last southbound express stop on the L&N (and from there you took the Southern Pacific west through the cowboy country and beyond the Rocky Mountains and across the elbow cactus deserts to Los Angeles, California, the city of red-tiled stucco haciendas and of pineapple-yellow sunsets and the sad sailor-boy music of Hawaiian guitars and ukeleles).

Another thing was whenever they used to say Nu-Awleens or Nu-Awlns or Gnawlins or Neweleens what you saw without even closing your eyes was a wide-open babylonian city of sin, a crescent seaport town of french lace wrought-iron and palmettos, of sporting-house madams, and incense-burning hoodoo madams, and coke sniffers in a part of town known as Algiers.

In Mobile, which after all was a very old French Catholic town too, the Mardi Gras season came only once a year, like Xmas. But in songs and barbershop tales it used to be as if in New Orleans (where they buried people in vaults on top of the ground and came back from the funeral with a brass band playing ragtime music) there was a carnival every night.

Then later on you came to realize that they also called it an open city for other reasons. Population-wise it was a Creole town, a rainbow city, a rainbow-crescent City of All Nationalities. Not that you ever quite got the impression that it was as wide open as San Francisco still was in the days of Jack Johnson. But not only was it by all odds the least segregated of Deep South cities, it had also been for a very long historical time much more cosmopolitan in many ways than were such schoolbook-sanctified capitals of Liberty and Justice for All as Boston and Philadelphia.

Nowadays, of course, it is open in many ways that it never was open before. So this time you put up at a premier-class hotel and you eat at the most famous of the French Quarter restaurants. But not only as you did in Atlanta and Mobile and will do in Greenville and Memphis but also as you and any number of other ex-servicemen and expense-account travelers have long since become accustomed to doing when the budget permits. Because you're back this time not only from up-town Manhattan and not only from Manhattan at large but also from Rome and Athens and Istanbul; Paris and London and Madrid; Amsterdam and Copenhagen and elsewhere.

But even so, what you really wish you had enough time to find the right people to ask about is the part of town you remember from the old fireside sagas and barbershop chronicles about Robert Charles and Aaron Harris and Black Benny and Lady Mary Jack the Bear. Which is also the part of town that musicians like Buddy Bolden and King Oliver and Papa Celestin and old loud wolfing Jelly Roll Morton came from. Not to mention Louis Armstrong who was already into his big-league stride even in those days and was already hitting solid gold and liquid silver notes higher than the Empire State Building as easily as shooting marbles.

All you have time to do this trip, however, is pop into

a few nearby places (including such landmarks as you can find along Rampart Street). Actually the main reason you are stopping over in New Orleans this time is to make a side trip to Covington for an afternoon visit with Walker Percy. Then one day and overnight in Greenville and one day in Memphis. Then back north by east to The Apple. Beale Street to Lenox Avenue in astrojet shuttle time. Then the tilted sandtable panorama you are sometimes lucky enough to get banking and letting down into the La Guardia landing pattern. Then the skyline above FDR Drive, and Harlem River as you see it from Hell Gate and through the latticework of Triborough Bridge. Then finally midtown in the twilight from the chinaberry seat above 132nd Street.

Perhaps the most widely repeated detail about the personal life of Walker Percy, the author of *The Moviegoer* and *The Last Gentleman,* is the fact that as a boy he was a favorite nephew and sometime household ward of William Alexander Percy of the Greenville, Mississippi, Percys, perhaps best known by outsiders as the Percys of *Lanterns on the Levee,* the recollections of a delta planter's very cavalier book-reading son, namely Will Alexander himself. Nor is this sort of detail merely another bit of Deep South Society-page trivia, not in this instance. Some threadbare elements of pseudo-antebellum snobbishness are there to be sure; but even so the family reference is legitimized by the all but inescapable implication that William Alexander Percy, the lawyer turned poet, is precisely the "real ancestor" in whose footsteps young Walker, the doctor turned novelist, elected to follow. The uncle's influence may or may not be unmistakable, but it is nonetheless there, even if stronger in matters of style than of content. Moreover, had he lived to read *The Moviegoer* not only would the ancestral uncle have had reason to be proud, he might even have shown a wee bit of genteel envy for good measure.

Had he lived to read some of his no less cosmopolitan than Southern nephew's commentaries on Negroes and on the Civil Rights movement however, he is likely to have been somewhat bemused to say the least. Not that on occasion he himself didn't indulge in such yankee-trumping declarations as: *"Any little boy who was not raised with little Negro children might as well not have been raised at all."* But when you got down to the question of black adults as full-fledged fellow citizens Uncle Will Alex for all his catholicity of taste and all his verse-oriented humility before man's fate, was a paternalistic old delta plantation racist to the end of his days.

Once he got going on black grown folks his incomparably fond memories of Nain, the warm, sweet-smelling, "divinely café au lait" teenage black mammy who nursed him, and of Skillet, his first boon companion and craw-fish-hunting buddy, are completely superseded by such self-bullshitting snobbishness as: *"Apparently there is something peculiarly Negroid in the Negro's attitude toward and aptitude for crimes of violence. He seems to have resisted, except on the surface, our ethics and to*

*have rejected our standards. Murder, thieving, lying, vio-
lence—I sometimes suspect the Negro doesn't regard
these as crimes or sins, or even regrettable occurrences.
He commits them casually with no apparent feeling of
guilt. White men similarly delinquent become soiled or
embittered or brutalized. Negroes are as charming after
as before a crime. . . ."*

Such neo-Marse-John-isms as: *"How is it possible for
the white man to communicate with people* [who believe in voodoo], *whom imagination kills and fantasy
makes impotent, who thieve like children and murder
ungrudgingly as small boys fight?"*

And, perhaps inevitably, such traditional Deep South
white ass-out hang-ups as: *"Every black buck in the
south has gone or will go to Chicago, where it is not only
possible but inexpensive to sleep with a white whore.
Likewise there are Negro bellboys in Southern hotels
frequented by white whores. . . . In former generations
when the taboo was unquestioned, Southern women felt
a corresponding obligation so to conduct themselves that
any breach of the taboo was unthinkable."*

The context of which, of course, was: *"The Negro
not having assimilated the white man's ethics, giving
only lip-service to the white man's morality, must for his
own peace and security accept wholeheartedly the white
man's mores and taboos. And the one sacred taboo,
assumed to be Southern but actually and universally
Anglo-Saxon, is the untouchability of white women by
Negro men."*

Then, in summary: *"I would say to the Negro: before
demanding to be a white man socially and politically,*

learn to be a white man morally and intellectually—and to the white man, the black man is our brother, a younger brother, not adult, not disciplined, but tragic, pitiful, and lovable. Act as his brother and be patient."

Thus old marse Will Alex, now in the cold cold clay where complexions are forgotten along with profits and losses and pecking orders. But not Walker, who in the following statement about adulthood in a letter to *Harper's* Magazine sounds as if his real uncle was named not Will Alex at all but Remus or Lucas Beauchamp or Sam Fathers: "*... as one thinks about the perennial adolescence of the American intellectual community ... it suddenly occurs to one: maybe it is the likes of* [Ralph] *Ellison we've needed all along. That is to say, maybe the American intellectual will not grow up until the Negro intellectual shows him how."*

Nor can it be argued that uncle and nephew are closer together in their conceptions of the dynamics of social change in the South. And while medicine is no less realistic than law there is still some irony in the fact that it is Walker the erstwhile doctor, not Will Alexander the lawyer, whose political insight reflects the old downhome seed-store, feed-store plus courthouse-square sense of local actualities at its pragmatic best. As a matter of fact the following statement may well have been written by a nephew who read his books in someplace like, say, Gavin Stevens' law office in Faulkner's Jefferson, rather than in the library of old Percy house in Greenville: "*Changing men's hearts has nothing to do with it. The Negro will vote without difficulty in Mississippi as soon as those who would stop him know they will be put in jail if they try."*

So no Civil Rights catechism for Walker Percy either. Nor do you have to declare your own articles of faith. But then it is almost always likely to be the all too sympathetic northern do-gooder, not the so-called reconstructed Southerner, who invites you to join him on some social occasion only to bore the hell out of you with questions that often are as tastelessly personal as political and as fatuous as they are naive. Seldom do such Southerners as extend social invitations to you so presume upon their prerogatives as hosts, either to impress you with their liberal credentials and their philanthropic good will or to instruct you on the essential nature of blackness, the fundamental implications of black experience, and the social imperatives and political priorities of black organizations.

No, as it is easy enough to find out from relatives who work as domestics, on such occasions down South, the traditional proprieties and amenities of Big House hospitality apply no less to you than to anybody else. You are presented to the folks present (some of course may be discreetly absent); you are served good whiskey; you are shown the sights both indoors and out; and what with all the easy innuendoes of "Hey we know your folks and y'all know some of ours, don't we?" the talk is likely to be anything but condescending.

Nor will there be any such other guests as are likely to forget their best company manners. Not that you may not be running the risk of being ambushed on your way home. But not by any of the guests, though some may look the other way the next time you pass on a downtown street. But in this they are not terribly different from some of their northern betters. In any case it is in the northern not the Southern drawing room that the other guests are most likely to insist that you explain why the hell you're there instead of in Harlem.

Furthermore, as hung up about black sexuality as far too many white Southerners so obviously have been (apparently ever since the days of the stud male slave), when a white Southerner asks if a reformer wants his sister to marry a Negro the implications of his questions go beyond his traditional Peeping Tom nightmares. Because no matter what else he may be hung up on, the white Southerner is also asking if the yankee do-gooder is really prepared for—or even conscious of—some of the inevitable personal and private consequences of his ever-so bighearted public gestures in interest of social reform. *"O.K., fellow, you're so hot to trot on desegregating them schools and such, to help the underdog and the like, but what about when the black underdog suddenly begins to act like black is equal enough to be a normal part of the family? How 'bout that fellow?"*

Naturally, the Southerner has his own chickenshit reasons for putting this kind of old stuff in the game. But when the liberal crusader retorts that questions about love affairs and marriage are irrelevant to the question of open institutions in the United States the white Southerner is quite certain that the northerner is copping out. And even more certain, needless to add, are all homefolks you've ever heard discussing such things. *Hell that's all right about the relevance why don't they just answer the simple ass damn question. Do you or don't you, would you, or wouldn't you try to stop her. Are you or aren't you as hung up on the possibility of black in-laws as Southerners—or perhaps even a little more so, since the Southerner's notorious racism is often more concerned with public decorum than with private behavior?* Somebody once declared that when you come right down to intimate personal contacts, the Southerner is likely to be lying when he says he is a racist and the northerner is likely to be lying when he professes not to be one.

At any rate when Walker Percy, looking somewhat more like a book-reading moviegoer than a delta planter's son's nephew, calls for you at your Canal Street hotel in downtown New Orleans, your radar, which you rate second to none, registers Normal then Cordial then Welcome. And in no time at all the two of you are breezing along the blue and gray causeway across Lake Ponchartrain toward Covington, exchanging anecdotes about New York: the Manhattan he remembers from the time when he was a young doctor dissecting corpses at Bellevue; the one you sometimes recall not only from the Harlem in which Ralph Ellison was working on *Invisible Man,* but also from NYU, Greenwich Village, the Public Library, and the Gotham Book Mart, the New York year you always recall when you hear such records as say, "Night in Tunisia," "Ornithology" and "Yardbird Suite." Nor is the point of the exchange to illustrate the distance of his Manhattan from Harlem. It is rather for the express purpose of making a mutual acknowledgment of a downhome angle of vision and sensibility. Not that either he or you are in the least unaware of your numerous differences.

But to be conscious of dissimilarities is not necessarily to be divided by them. Some self-styled color-blind white Americans who obviously assume that they must pretend to ignore differences in order to avoid conflict only add hypocrisy to already existing complications. Moreover, if some of the differences between two given people are racial, which is mostly to say a matter of several physical features, others are mostly personal; and human nature being what it is, whatever its habitat, there is always an outside chance that any two people even from opposite ends of the earth will find in each other more similarities of personal interest and emphasis upon which to build a friendship or at least a cordial acquaintanceship, than race-oriented differences to separate them into antithetical factions. Indeed, enthnocentrism notwithstanding, seldom is racial or even national identity alone enough to provide for an acquaintanceship comparable to one growing out of mutual personal interests.

In any case one fundamental assumption underlying your visit with Walker Percy as with Edwin Yoder and Joe Cumming and the rest goes without saying: Two book-oriented Southerners, one Afro-brown and one Anglo-caucasian have at least as much to talk about as two downhome baseball players for instance, whose physical features and historical extractions are similarly different from and similarly similar to each other.

It is Ernest Hemingway not William Faulkner who provides the keynote and vamp-in this time. In reply to a casual inquiry about works-in-progress you sketch the objectives of *The Hero and the Blues*, a recently completed draft of literary notes in which you use the *nada-*

conscious, ritual-oriented master craftsman as one of three primary literary touchstones for a blues-idiom–derived frame of reference, if not poetics, for the kind of fiction you are trying to write. But then aren't the preoccupations of *The Moviegoer* closer to the Faulkner of *Mosquitoes* and *The Wild Palms*, than to *Light in August* and *Absalom, Absalom!?* You for your part had placed the Faulkner of *Mosquitoes* and *Pylon* and *The Green Bough* in the context of T. S. Eliot's *The Waste Land* and Hemingway's *The Sun Also Rises*, long before the interview in which he called himself a failed poet.

Naturally you have absolutely no intention whatsoever of going into that sort of thing at such a time. Nor is there any need to do so, for such is the enthusiasm of Walker Percy's immediate response to the mention of Hemingway that by the time the new-smelling T-bird pulls into Covington your hastily sketched conception of the *Nada*-Confrontation Hero has provided a functional context within which the talk has included the existentialist notion of the absurd and the Malraux-Pascal image of man's fate. All of which, you realize later, is directly related to an aspect of southernness that C. Vann Woodward may be getting at when he refers to the northern illusion that "history is something unpleasant that happens to other people," and then declares that nothing about Southern history is conducive to the theory that the South is "the darling of divine providence."

The first sight of the house in Covington takes you back to the *petit château* you and your literary friends including James Baldwin used to ride out to visit in Mary Painter's Renault and sometimes swim near on

Sunday afternoons during that first summer in Paris. There is something about its cozy scale and the somewhat formal layout of the front lawn that also evokes such undergraduate textbook names as Madame de Staël, Madame de Sévigné—or is it the bewigged and bepowdered Agnes Morehead?

But what the moss-and-cypress setting along with the taste of the Louisiana bayou-scented air also takes you back to at the same time is the Spanish Main that you grew up hearing about and reading about. So you enter the fine drawing room thinking in terms of bayou *châteaux* instead of Big Houses and plantation houses this time. And being of precisely the same generation of moviegoers as Walker himself, part of you is naturally disposed to believe that every excellent old piece of furniture and bric-a-brac in sight was originally imported by buccaneers under the direct command of Akim Tamiroff.

For all the swashbuckling romance that the casks and cut-glass decanters of ruby port and golden madeira were so much a part of in the old technicolor sea and treasure-coast movies however, what you choose to sip this time is Tennessee bourbon (superimposing Charlton Heston's Andy Jackson at the Battle of New Orleans upon Lionel Barrymore's Old Hickory, the husband of the Gorgeous Hussy). And what you spend the rest of the bayou-soft, delta-blue afternoon sitting out in the backyard on the bayou marina landing watching the bayou water skiers and talking mostly about is fiction, Deep South fiction. About Shelby Foote, author of *Tournament, Follow Me Down*, and *Shiloh*, who is now into the third thick volume of a nonfiction narrative of the Civil War; about the late Flannery O'Connor, Eudora Welty, Carson McCullers, and Truman Capote.

Then about Robert Penn Warren and of course Faulkner. But what is said about William Faulkner this time is not simply in celebration of his considerable talent and remarkable achievement but rather to acknowledge some of the very serious esthetic problems he creates for younger Southern writers. The big thing, the two of you agree, is not to be overwhelmed by him; to profit from his achievement, which, as Hemingway once said about his own, is now in the public domain, without mistaking his special point of view as your own. "Man, Shelby and I talk about this sometimes and he says that stuff can get to be downright pernicious. With Ellison, of course, it is a different thing if you know what I mean."

About Thomas Wolfe he says at one point: "I've re-read some of it and I'm afraid it doesn't . . . When I read it a long time ago . . ." Later when you mention Reynolds Price, William Goyen, Ernest J. Gaines, and Fred Chapell he adds Cormac MacCarthy: "Have you read *The Orchard Keeper* and *Outer Dark?* He can write. Of course he's got his problems with Faulkner too, but I think you'll find him very interesting."

Nor is the conversation any less Southern or one bit less fiction-oriented when you suddenly remember to ask if having spent some time in Alabama he happens to know the difference between what you used to call the mulberry bush and what you also knew as the mulberry tree. You haven't been able to find it in Rickett's compendious *Wildflowers of the Southeastern United States.*

He does know the difference. Or rather he is certain about the absolute difference in the berries. But not the names. In consequence however, back in New York, a week or so later you receive an envelope containing a leaf and the following note: *"Al, is this the leaf? If it is it's Spanish mulberry—has a purple berry. Shelby was disappointed not to see you."* So now you remember. Because in Mobile they used to call them *French* mulberries. When you said mulberry tree you were talking about the kind of berries you eat. When you said mulberry bush you were talking about the pale purple almost tasteless kind you swished like play-buckshot.

As for the radar indications of relative freedom from traditional Confederate hang-ups, they remain consistently clear of the alert zone throughout the visit. So, for whatever a Buster Brown voucher may be worth in these media-conditioned times of so much grab-bag revolutionary gobbledegook, your response to the old often only visual question ("Whose and what kind is this one?") is that it is probably quite safe to consider Walker Percy a pretty good one too. Yes, for all that many of his most fondly cherished boyhood memories may well involve an uncle whose book jacket profile you for one imagined Sidney Poitier slapping in that highly improbable but ever so gleefully and liberalistically masochistic greenhouse incident in Norman Jewison's movie *In the Heat of the Night.*

Indeed for all that what the old Saenger Theatre peanut-gallery–derived part of you sometimes fantasizes is a scenario in which the likes of old man Will Alex is shown, lantern in hand, getting his paternalistic ass kicked from one end of the levee to the other by a cigar-smoking, golden-smiling Jack Johnson—looking jelly bean, wearing a silk candy-striped gambler's shirt with sleeve garters, a tan Kingfish derby, pegtop pants and two-toned pointy-toed shoes, it is precisely *Walker* Percy's freedom from condescension that you are inclined to vouch for first of all.

Nor for all your first-hand downhome experience of interracial violence do you find it altogether less urgent for him or Red Warren or Vann Woodward or Ed Yoder or Joe Cumming to be free of such northern-style tolerance as is only insidious benevolence than from traditional Southern-style hysteria. Anyway so far you have seen nothing to indicate that he is likely to exchange the agenbite of his inwit for the agit-prop of such New York City nitwits as are for a revolution of brotherhood, love, and racial separatism at the same time.

But, in the final analysis, since the primary reason that you are in contact with Walker Percy is that he is a writer whose work you consider significant, what more in all fairness (and indeed in all hard-headed calculation) can you ask of him than that he bring to all issues the same ambivalent literary sense of human complexity that characterizes *The Moviegoer?*

David L. Cohn may or may not have been the second generation carpetbagger-become-dilettante that some exasperated Tuskegeans used to insist that he had all the earmarks of. But in *God Shakes Creation*, which came out seven years before *Lanterns on the Levee* and could have been called *Darkness on the Delta*, he did strike you as being ever so eager to pass himself off as a delta planter's snobbish son. Whoever or whatever he was or fancied himself to be in the flesh, however, on paper he almost always came across as a book-reading redneck (which he wasn't either) trying to write his way into the inner sanctum sanctorum of white supremacy.

Sometimes William Alexander Percy could almost take his position in the status quo for granted. At such times he felt secure enough to indulge himself in the form of condescension known as *noblesse oblige*. But it was almost always as if Cohn were a book-reading and airs-taking "town" Snopes who had to be forever looking for new ways to convince himself that black people were inherently inferior to the white people he chose to identify with. Nowhere are the hypocrisies and pretensions that this often led to more apparent than in his statements on Topic One.

Thus: "*Wherever men have lived in the world sexual relations have existed between conqueror and conquered, invader and invaded, master and slave. It was thus that*" [*so and so and so*] "*and the white men of the south took Negro women as concubines during slavery and after freedom. . . . The white man of the Delta was merely writing his chapter in the long record of the white race throughout the world wherever it has come in contact with colored peoples of a simpler culture or weaker fiber.*"

And yet: "*Rape is a crime shockingly abhorrent to men all over the world.*"

Now, that being the case, Cohn's chapter-writing delta white man suddenly becomes: "*A creature of conventions and inhibitions. He must consider public opinion and the force of law. Marriage, the child and the family are still basic units of the society in which he moves. His religion casts a shadow over eros.*"

From which for David L. Cohn it somehow just naturally follows that "*The Negro on the other hand is sexually completely free and untrammeled. 'W'en I wants me a woman, I gets me a woman.' Sexual desire is raw and crude and strong. It is to be satisfied when and wherever it arises. It is not embroidered with roses and raptures of romantic love. It does not proceed tortuously through devious detours of flirtation but flies straight to its mark with the blind compulsion and devouring intensity of a speeding bullet.*"

So now therefore: "*The great inflexible taboo of sexual relationships in the Delta is that there shall not be under any circumstances, 'a sexual relationship between a white woman and a Negro.'*" But of course as for the sexual exploitation of black women by the conqueror and master: "*The women were on the whole willing and even eager to assume a sexual relationship with him and they were quite venal in their attitude.*"

But behold the conqueror once again: "*The white man of the Delta living among masses of Negroes overwhelmingly superior in number and well armed, fears them only in one aspect. He does not fear bodily harm* to himself, nor an armed uprising. There has never been such an uprising in the Delta. He does, however, fear sexual attacks upon his women."

Nor was old David L.'s hang-up any less central to his conception of things when *God Shakes Creation* was expanded and republished as *Where I Was Born and Raised* in 1948: "[We] *must acknowledge that the race question is primarily insoluble because in the conscious or unconscious minds of Southern whites it is a blood or sexual question,*" which wraps things up very nicely but not very neatly since it implies that the steady stream of Mississippi-born mulattoes has nothing to do with blood and sex.

In all events what you are as keenly aware of as anything else as you dial the *Delta Democrat Times* from the Downtowner Motel is the following background fact of everyday life and of letters in Greenville, Mississippi: this Hodding Carter, whom you will soon be meeting, not only enjoyed a very close, warm, and enduring friendship with William Alexander Percy, who was indeed his chief benefactor during the early days of the *Democrat Times*, but was only slightly less chummy with David L. Cohn to boot—in fact it was Cohn who put him in touch with Percy in the first place.

Of course, you are also no less aware or appreciative of the fact that nothing about *The Lower Mississippi, Where Main Street Meets the River* or *First Person Rural, The Angry Scar,* or anything else of his that you recall smacks either of planterly dilettantism or of carpetbagging opportunism gone to decadent racism. But then the point

is not that you have ever had reason to suspect Hodding
Carter of writing with forked quill. That is not the point
at all. The point is that the Buster Brown alert system is
properly calibrated and properly zeroed in. The point is
that what really counts is the feedback from the Deep
South zone you have entered now.

Meanwhile the tentative classification of Hodding
Carter on your voucher scale over the years has been
militant moderate, and the good part about his militancy is that when he came out for something he was
willing to fight for it. But the bad part about being
moderate is that it has permitted him to stomach too
many unspeakable outrages both physical and intellectual over the years. Indeed, on the question of racial fair
play he has sometimes come alarmingly close to equat-
ing northern hypocrisy with Southern mob violence,
which is not to describe his intentions, only the implications of some of the positions he has sometimes taken
with regard to the priorities and urgencies of black
citizenship.

Anyway it is Hodding Carter that you have stopped
off to meet at this point and all you intend to vouch
for this time is how he strikes you in person as of today.

But as things turn out, what with him not yet re-
covered from a recent siege of a recurring ailment, and
what with young Hod, his successor at the *Delta Democrat Times*, having to rush off to do his last day bit for
the Charles Evers campaign, the one you spend most of
your visit talking to is not Hodding himself but his wife
Betty; whose pattern on the detector system, incidentally, yields nothing whatsoever to any moviegoer's image

of the Katharine Hepburn who used to go so well with Spencer Tracy in the heyday of his square-jawed, two-fisted editorship.

Hodding is there and in good enough spirits considering the state of his health, but it is Betty, who also reminds you of Rose Styron and Ralph Ellison's wife Fanny, who drives the station wagon and serves as the best of all possible writer-oriented guides on the town, the levee, the Indian mounds, and finally the Carter estate. It is also Betty who begins by saying, "So now tell us something about your assignment. Dave Halberstam just told us to expect you." So it is to her, not directly to Hodding, that you sketch your outline of the seed-store–feed-store courthouse-square dimension of Southern sensibility this time (and later she feeds it back to your complete satisfaction in introducing you first to Mrs. Jesse Brent and to Mrs. Roger Generelley).

It is also to her that you say: "Every time I suggest that the somewhat younger white Southern journalists who best represent what I mean are in a very real sense heirs to and extensions of the best qualities of such older guys as Jonathan Daniels and Ralph McGill, somebody almost always says: And Hodding Carter. So here I am stopping by to see y'all. Willie sends regards and so does Walker."

"Willie is doing a good job up there," Hodding says. "How does he like it?" ("Tell him to watch out up there," somebody elsewhere has already said, "they'll have him so he won't know whether he's going or coming.") But what he is most talkative about from time to time is local Indian history, the geography of the

Mississippi River, and the delights of catfish eating. But when Betty points out examples of local progress toward desegregation he nods his approval and expresses his pleasure at the fact that it is proceeding with so little friction. As for the several books that he has under way it is Betty who says that he is writing beautifully and moving right along in spite of the fact that he is able to work only a few hours each day.

So what you come away vouching for this time is the fact that the Betty that Hodding wrote about with so much astonished affection in *Where Main Street Meets the River* is in as fine form as ever. As for Hodding himself, your one-day impression of him in person was essentially compatible with the one you had formed from his books and articles over the years, which was that for all the shortcomings inherent in the whiteness of his special Southern partisanship he was never quite as unmindful of the immediate implication of the nation's deeper interests as some of his closest personal friends so obviously were.

You keep trying but are unable to get Shelby Foote on the phone, but what you also do in the meantime is explore downtown Memphis, and have yourself a solid expense-account lunch at the Peabody Hotel wondering what the reaction of the management would be to a suggestion from, say, Willie Morris or Albert Erskine that they name a bar for William Faulkner or maybe a lounge for *Sanctuary*; wondering also how much historical fact there is in the old legend about how the social status of white Southerners on the make sometimes used to depend on whether or not the Negro headwaiter there recognized them, called their names with just the right inflection and seated them promptly or ignored them and their guests until all the best tables were occupied.

After lunch you look at the river from bluffs that Mark Twain, the apprentice riverboatman like Abe Lincoln the flatboatman before him, saw on his way down to New Orleans. Then you stroll along Beale Street, the old stamping ground of W. C. Handy, whose blues about it and about Memphis in the days of Boss Crump and about St. Louis, the metropolis up the river, represent a dimension of the national experience, character, and sensibility that not even the best fiction of Mark Twain and William Faulkner makes one adequately conscious of. In point of fact the "St. Louis Blues" is a veritable national anthem, the rendering of which probably stirs some very old interior place of more Americans than does "The Star-Spangled Banner." After all, what you feel (whether with pride or irony) when you hear "The Star-Spangled Banner" is mostly those schoolboy things that go with the flag and with the illustrations you remember from grade-school history books. But what the music of the "St. Louis Blues" evokes, whether along with brownskin goosepimples or along with pale faces and red ears, is the actual texture of American places and occasions that exist in your personal recollection. Anyway hearing "The Star-Spangled Banner" in a foreign country may or may not make most Americans downright homesick, but you are willing to bet that hearing the "St. Louis Blues" would. Nor would you have excluded the likes of William Alexander Percy and David L. Cohn.

By the time you come to the park named for him, you also remember that among the blues that W. C. Handy either composed or transcribed was also one about Aunt Hagar. Sometimes as in the recording by Louis Armstrong it was called "Aunt Hagar's Blues"; and sometimes as in "Erskine Hawkins Plays W. C. Handy for Dancing," it is called "Aunt Hagar's Children." But it is music that goes with having a downhome good time no matter what it is called. *You close your eyes remembering what Louis did with the words and how Erskine's arranger scored the music and suddenly you are all the way back to the old fireside times, when you yourself used to become one of Aunt Hagar's rawhide roustabouts anytime you wanted to and used to come up from the old steamboat landing to the goodtime places along Beale Street doing that sporty patent-leather limp walk that such wide-eyed boy-scout yokels as Tom Sawyer and Huck Finn couldn't even begin to hold a candle to.*

What you see when you open your eyes again is the view of the updated downtown Memphis skyline that you get looking across Handy Park from the long-since rundown oldness of that part of Beale Street as of now. So Mister Buster Brown that you were brought up to never cease to be, what you feel is that very special old sensation of urgency that you inherited along with those whose restless struggles are at last adding up to the local civil-rights confrontations. But what you also find yourself all the more deeply engaged by is that which Beale Street symbolizes for you in spite of all the shabbiness, some of which was always there anyway: *Music for good times earned in adversity. A sound track for an affirmative life-style riffed in resilient blue steel from the least congenial of all American circumstances.*

If you could only find a way to make enough civil-rights spokesmen and leaders realize that there is an immediate and fundamental connection between all that and the sociopolitical objectives to which you and they like all other bright-eyed Misters Buster Brown—each in his own way—were eternally committed. If you could only get enough of them to consider that the rhetoric of welfare militancy currently so popular among them may only add up to an overreaction to a lot of second-rate folklore of white supremacy that is no less vicious than that of the old William Alexander Percys and David L. Cohns, for all the scientific terminology it is couched in these days. If you can only get them to see that they don't have to play themselves and the cause cheap just to make a case for safeguards and benefits that the constitution already guarantees as their birthright. You fight for such things. You don't go around putting on the poormouth about them.

Nor is the problem simply only that somebody is deliberately betraying the cause. That never has been a major part of the problem. And much goes to show that those who are quick to imply that it is are only running off at the mouth without thinking or else are trying to bootleg some old self-styled Emperor Jones stuff into the game. (Some Buster Browns do become Afro-Carib

Emperors Mac Brown: *"Anybody don't do what I tell 'em is a part of my problem. Ain't nobody doing better than me but them that sold us all out to the white folks."*) Bullshit. HNIC Bullshit, Black strawboss bullshit.

No, as you have now come to see it, the primary problem is not combat security (not yet at any rate) but rather the mobilization and utilization of existing human resources. The problem is how to evolve sociopolitical tactics and strategies that are truly indigenous to and compatible with the dynamics of U.S. Negro life style. Because until somebody does, the so-called masses are not likely to become very deeply involved no matter how earnest your appeals—even to their self-interest. Take the example of Martin Luther King, whose name is now also a part of Memphis. For all the justification of his theories of nonviolence that he found in Thoreau and Gandhi, it was probably the charismatic dynamics of the downhome church that most of his followers, even the white ones, many of them non-Christian, were responding to.

If you could only get enough spokesmen and leaders to consider the possibility that the dynamics inherent in the blues idiom might be extended further than King was able to take those derived from the downhome church. Not that you did not celebrate the effectiveness of King's methods, as far as they went. But as a political device they were limited as all moral outcry is bound to be. So what you hoped was that the blues idiom, *being of its essence a SECULAR form of existential improvisation,* could produce something better.

If you could only get a few key spokesmen and leaders to help you tee off on some of those hypocritical white do-gooders and one-up-men who misrepresent it as being something you should either outgrow or be cured of. If you could do that maybe you could also get a few of them to realize that when they confused Uncle Remus with Uncle Tom they were probably allowing themselves to be faked out by superficial political rhetoric instead of relying on their actual experience. Maybe you could even get a few to realize what they were doing when they let some third-rate con man jargonize them into denying Aunt Hagar—as if who if not Aunt Hagar is the source of all stone foxiness! (*"Man, if you go to the Waldorf to see Lena Horne and don't realize that what she's riffing on is Aunt Hagar, you're wasting your money!"*)

You also make your way over to Third and Vance streets and the Lorraine Motel where Martin Luther King was murdered by sniper fire (you were backstage at Carnegie Hall with Duke when the word came, brought by Jim Jenson of WCBS-TV news, this time in person, wearing a moviegoer's Burberry trench coat and shaking his head and adding "some goddam white guy and he got away"). So what you find yourself wondering about en route back to Memphis International for the final leg of the flight back to New York is whether the ill-fated Memphis Confrontations that cost King his life (and the movement its most magnetic spokesman and leader) would have turned out as badly if King and his staff men and well-wishers and assorted hangers-on had been just a little less hopeful about the impact of moral out-

cry as such, however massive its volume, and a good deal
more alert to the political facts of life. It was, you concede, only natural for a very sincere minister and church
folks and welfare-oriented activists to gear their methods
to appeals to compassion. But that was the point. Just
how deep into the complications of things does your
commitment to the cause go? Do you love your people
enough to do some dirty work in order to bring them
some good? Or easier than that. Do you love your people
enough to pay the necessary research dues for the cause?
What did Max Weber, whose definition of politics as
the use of power you were riffing on, say: Only those
who realize how awful and self-destructive and so on
people can be and still pay dues for the privilege of ad-
ministering their affairs truly have talent for politics.
Something like that. Max Weber from whom all the
cocktail party chatter about charisma is probably derived
via C. Wright Mills and Talcott Parsons.

Anyway one thing that was probably wrong with the
Memphis Confrontation was that it was, as they say,
already another ball game before Memphis. It was a
new ball game as soon as they passed that voting rights
bill. Maybe what was lacking was that King was too
much of a Christian idealist to realize and capitalize on
the fact that his downhome church-oriented nonviolence was really a form of political jujitsu. Perhaps the
most subtle ever attempted in the whole history of the
country. Maybe he was too nice to admit even to himself that he was really provoking the opposition to violence for the express purpose of tricking them into
using their own strength against themselves; and yet what

was he forever saying if not: *"Oh brothers and sisters let us now turn the other cheek with love and wait for Lyndon Johnson to follow the lead of Jack and Bobby and federalize the National Guard right out from under these crackers."*

King may not have been able to see himself in that role even if he had lived to be ninety. But there was hardly any way for any power technician to mistake what really happened at Birmingham and Selma. *They knew damn well that they couldn't be outgunned but what had happened was they had been outsmarted, outmaneuvered.* Any feed-store-seed-store courthouse-square power technician could figure that out and know what to change the game to. All they had to do was start cashing in on all that expensive exposure somebody had been providing free for any loudmouth hustler out to cop himself some cheap note, playing the black booger man waving a BB gun and striking matches in the woodpile. Once they got the jive-time war whoopers going, all they had to do was sit tight and wait for the media-oriented tom-toms and war dances, and any American crossroads-store power technican could tell you what the name of the game is and whose ball and bat it is going to be played with.

It could be called the Friend of Indians Game (in which "no-good" white men provide the Indians with just enough guns and ammo to set them on the warpath and into ambush). But it is usually called Shooting Fish in a Barrel. And the thing about it is that not only will the welfare foundations go for it; so will the ever so nonviolent Compassion Corps. All they need is reassurance that red-blooded white Americans would never actually shoot the mullet-heads once they have been tricked into the barrel. A few squeamish liberals might balk. But there will be plenty of New York intellectuals who will reason that a gas oven is not actually a gas oven until you actually light the gas.

All you need claim for blues-idiom–oriented political behavior at this point is that it is less given to self-defeating self-righteousness than is moral outcry rhetoric. All you need to point out is that when the self-righteous people you know turn to violence they seem to spend so much time justifying their right to pick up the gun that they forget to learn how to shoot, as if the rightness of the cause were in itself a functional substitute for combat readiness and combat intelligence. All you need to say is that blues-oriented people are conditioned to confront the facts of life.

As the airport-bound limousine rolls on out of the city limits what you remember is the news reports of the fiasco that the first Memphis Confrontation became. That is why there had to be a Second Memphis Confrontation. So it is also why Martin Luther King was back in Memphis on the day he was shot. You remember how well things had gone in Birmingham where the political jujitsu worked well enough to zap Bull Conner after all those legendary years. (Indeed, what you for your part like best to remember King doing was not speaking of hopes and dreams on the Washington Mall —as good as he was that day—but making the rounds to all the toughest Birmingham joints saying in so many words: "*Cool it for the cause, brothers. Old Bull ain't going to know what hit him. Old Bull going to be feeling them cattle prods long after they become jokes to us.*"

But he couldn't make it work in Memphis either time. And at least one reason why he couldn't was that by that time quite a number of his troops were as pre-occupied with proving to the media that they were not a bunch of Mama's boys as with improving their economic and political condition. Once Big Daddy Moynihan's notorious monograph *The Negro Family* got the ever so committed and compassionate media going on all that matriarchy stuff King was bound to have more and more trouble trying to get media-oriented window-breaking warwhoopers to play it oriental-cool. Anyway, with all due respect to the fact that Martin Luther King appealed to the very best in his followers and adversaries alike, what you find yourself hoping now is that when the next national leader appears he will be a Hagar-endowed, Uncle Bud-Doc-Ned-Remus and Zack-wise, blues-oriented, poker-watchful political technician, (*who will be prepared to keep the faith of such foreparents as Frederick Douglass and Hariet Tubman among others, precisely because he will know that the thing about political objectives is that they require political strategy, who will know that the thing about all strategy is that it will come to nothing without tactical know-how. Not that he will not play the old moral-outcry jive line for whatever it is worth, but neither will he so misguide himself by his own propaganda as to commit his troops to any combat showdown before giving due consideration to the all too obvious fact that the thing about the force required* to achieve military objectives is of its very nature predicated upon military control, which is to say military discipline. Nor can the problem of insurgent troop morale and discipline for the long grind be separated from another problem: How do you alienate the great mass of Americans from their TV sets and the world of TV celebrities, especially in as much as your own status as spokesman leader is itself likely to be so largely dependent upon your TV ratings, since your most obvious competition is not the ever so shadowy establishment itself but the popular crime and western and variety programs, not to mention the headline sports events.)

Also, how do you alienate no-income people from the welfare system, and how do you get enough low-income people to choose the esoteric abstractions of Apocalypse propaganda over the ad-induced shopping sprees that are supported by an installment-plan credit system, and are perpetuated by the built-in obsolescence of the merchandise itself? Moreover, how do you sustain enough revolutionary momentum against a so-called Establishment that is not nearly so monolithic and recalcitrant as it is diverse and resilient—and is not only capable but is also very likely to riff your own stuff right back at you manifold? ("Right on out of it") Indeed, how do you prevent the so-called Establishment from turning your revolutionary slogans into its own pop promotion gimmicks—and reducing you to a media cliché in the bargain?

Then there are other and still other riddlesome considerations that perhaps nobody was ever any better qualified to wheel and deal with than some of the quick *brown, fox-crazy dog leaping briarpatch negotiators, whom you (like any number of schoolboy types, no doubt) have known, admired, and learned from for as long as you can remember.*

Anyway, the more you for one think about some of the theory-oriented leader/spokesmen who were already well on their way to media-prominence even before Martin Luther King's ill-fated mission to Memphis, the more you find yourself coming back to an old notion that it just might be his pragmatic orientation to the flesh-and-blood actualities of food, clothing, shelter, chance, and the contingencies of fellowship and romance that will best equip the blues-conditioned leader to keep the faith of his forefathers during these electro-media days of so much instantly amplified and conventionalized sound and furiousness. As for his own shortcomings, as of now they are (specific technical skills aside) mostly a matter of inadequate horizons of aspiration. In most instances all he would have to do is realize the national (and international) implications of his local achievements. Not that he has been playing himself cheap because he is deficient in self-esteem. It is rather his context of self-evaluation and appreciation that is too provincial, a matter which can be remedied with only the slightest turn of the screw, say no more than it took to get Willie Mays and Hank Aaron from the sandlots of Alabama to big-league superstardom.

As for the Ancestral Imperatives, now so frequently obscured by pretentious spokesmen overreacting to the Folklore of White Supremacy, what they require is very simple indeed: that you take care of the business at hand to the best of your ability, a business which begins, incidentally, not with historical romances about pre-American identities, but with such supermarket–city hall–monday morning matters as equal employment opportunities, equal protection under the law, equal access to civic services and living facilities, and adequate political representation.

As for the ancestral guidelines for the next national leader's conduct as a matinee idol, let him always remember at least this much about Uncle Jack the Bear: He was forever claiming to be nowhere precisely because he knew that there is all the difference in the world between being only faddish and being truly hip. *Man, ain't* NOTHING *happening, Man.*

You decide not to give Shelby Foote one final buzz from the airport, because once there you are already out of Memphis. You are in a sense already out of the South. You are already back in the national zone (and indeed, even in the intercontinental zone) and it would not be like talking to him down home anymore. It would be almost the same as calling from New York. It wouldn't even be very much like calling long distance from Harlem. It would be more like using a booth somewhere in midtown Manhattan with somebody standing outside wondering how much longer you're going to be there.

So you say maybe next time for Shelby Foote.

Meanwhile, all ante bellum joke twisting vouchers, identification papers, dog tags, signs, countersigns, and earmarks aside, what you come back up the country this time more concerned about than ever before is how to make more white intellectuals *not only down home but perhaps elsewhere first of all* more responsive to the fact that somebody has been keeping tab on them and their prettygoodness and godawfulness from such spyglass points as Lenox Terrace all along. Nor—for all the moral outcry rhetoric—has the field of surveillance ever really been restricted to interracial misbehavior. Indeed, the whole thing of tab keeping may well have begun with such captive African sages as passed the word on along to the young ones (whether in a whisper or by gestures and nods) that for all his high horses, Ole Marster got to put on his breeches one leg at a time just like everybody else; got to shake after number one and wipe after number two, for all his silk and satin; and for all his coaches and carriages and fine mansion, got to cry "Have Mercy" when the wagon come. Because he also got to end up six feet in the ground, and may or may not have had any more enjoyment than anybody else for all his wealth and power.

If you could only find a way to get some of *that* kind of old downhome folklore into the so-called National Dialogue about the quality of life in the United States.

EPILOGUE

Yes the also and also of all that also; because the oldness that you are forever going back again by one means or another to is not only of a place and of people but also and perhaps most often of the promises that exact the haze-blue adventuresomeness from the brown-skinned hometown boy in us all. There must by now be at least yes one thousand plus one or more tales all told of the underlying sameness; and whether retold by wine drinkers or beer drinkers or bootleg-whiskey drinkers, and whether in fire circles or by firesides, and whether in barbers' shoptalk or ten o'clock Latin or in blue-ribbon anthologies twelve-plus years advanced, the implications of self-definition, self-celebration, and perhaps not a little self-inflation and self-designation are nevertheless quite as obvious in each as for all and since forever: when you talking about somebody come from where us folks come from you talking about somebody come from somewhere. You talking about people been through something, you talking about somebody come out of something.

And is therefore ready for something. Because self-nomination after all has perhaps as much to do with promise and fulfillment as with anything else; and promise and fulfillment probably have at last as much to do with self-discipline as with anything else; and the thing about self-discipline (which is to say dedication which is to say commitment which is nothing if not self-obligation) is its conditioned unforgetfulness which is perhaps as good a reason as any why even the most frivolous-seeming good-time music of downhome-derived people so often sounds like so much rhapsodized thunder and syncopated lightning.

ABOUT THE AUTHOR

Albert Murray was born in Nokomis, Alabama, in 1916. He grew up in Mobile and was educated at Tuskegee Institute, where he later taught literature and directed the college theater. A retired major in the US Air Force, Murray has been O'Connor Professor of Literature at Colgate University, Visiting Professor of Literature at the University of Massachusetts in Boston, writer-in-residence at Emory University, and Paul Anthony Brick lecturer at the University of Missouri. His other works include *The Omni Americans* and *The Hero and the Blues* (essays), *Train Whistle Guitar* (a novel), *Stomping the Blues* (a history of the blues), *Good Morning Blues: The Autobiography of Count Basie* (as told to), and *The Spyglass Tree* (a novel).

Printed in the United States
by Baker & Taylor Publisher Services